THE ENCYCLOPAEDIA OF
EVERLASTINGS

THE ENCYCLOPAEDIA OF EVERLASTINGS

The Complete Guide to Growing, Preserving, and Arranging Dried Flowers

Barbara Radcliffe Rogers

Illustrations by
Kenneth Spengler, William S. Moye,
Roman Szolkowski, Mary Close,
Anita Marci

Weidenfeld & Nicolson
New York

A FRIEDMAN GROUP BOOK

Copyright © 1988 by Michael Friedman Publishing Group, Inc.

Published in the United States by
Weidenfeld & Nicolson, New York
A Division of Wheatland Corporation
10 East 53rd Street
New York, New York 10022

ISBN 1-55584-133-3

Library of Congress Cataloging-in-Publication Data

Rogers, Barbara Radcliffe.
     The encyclopaedia of everlastings : the complete guide to growing,
preserving, and arranging dried flowers / Barbara Radcliffe Rogers ;
illustrations by Kenneth Spengler ... [et al.]. — 1st ed.
          p.   cm.
     ''A Friedman Group book'' — T.p. verso.
     ISBN 1-555-84133-3
     1. Dried flower arrangement—Dictionaries. 2. Everlasting
flowers—Dictionaries. 3. Flowers—Drying—Dictionaries.
4. Plants—Drying—Dictionaries. 5. Flower gardening—Dictionaries.
6. Flower gardening—United States—Dictionaries. I. Title.
SB449.3.D7R63 1988   87–22514
745.9—dc19   CIP

THE ENCYCLOPAEDIA OF EVERLASTINGS
The Complete Guide to Growing,
Preserving, and Arranging Dried Flowers
was prepared and produced by
Michael Friedman Publishing Group
15 West 26th Street
New York, New York 10010

Editor: Nancy Kalish
Art Director: Mary Moriarty
Designer: Fran Waldmann
Production Manager: Karen L. Greenberg

Typeset by I, CLAVDIA Inc.
Color separations by Hong Kong Scanner Craft Company Ltd.
Printed and bound in Hong Kong by Leefung-Asco Printers Ltd.

First Edition 1988

10 9 8 7 6 5 4 3 2 1

DEDICATION

To Tim, whose first project in
each new home has been to surround
it with flowers—with appreciation for
twenty grand years of marriage

ACKNOWLEDGMENTS

It is common for authors to describe their books as labors of love. Honesty prompts me to admit that there was more love than labor lavished on this one. Or so it seemed. How can it be work to write about the blossoms that fill first my greenhouse, then my garden, and finally my house in a year-round profusion of color and fragrance?

One of the joys of flowers is that my whole family takes part. Tim has a boundless optimism that fills the greenhouse to overflowing by April; Lura's fingers seem specially made to handle tiny seedlings; Julie's practical eye oversees the progress of the flowers, from their growth in the field through the harvest; and my mother carefully sorts out the perfect rosebuds for tussy-mussies.

One other gardener remains to be thanked: a total stranger to whom I wrote for information on Hawaiian everlastings after reading of the lovely herbal wreaths she makes there. Her generous response came by return mail: a box full of carefully packaged and labeled samples of all her favorite dried plants. To Barbara Irwin of Heartscents in Hilo, Hawaii, goes my special lei of thanks.

TABLE OF CONTENTS

Introduction
Page 8

Methods of Plant Preservation
Page 9

Air-Drying
Watering
Pressing
Sand
Silica Gel

Methods and Tools for Arranging
Page 11

Garden Zone Map
Page 13

A Diagram of a Flower
Page 14

TABLE OF CONTENTS

KENNETH SPENGLER

INTRODUCTION

Flowers, like life's magic moments, are all the more precious for their brevity. A magnificent red poppy may burst into bloom, then fade in a single day. Even the continuously blooming annuals flower only for a season.

It is no wonder that we strive to preserve the bright beauty of growing things so that they may grace our homes long after they have faded from our gardens. This began centuries ago, when herbs and flowers were hung to dry for their medicinal and cosmetic values. At some point in these early stillrooms, it was perhaps noticed that some of the dried blossoms retained their shape and color. By the Victorian era, the procedures for drying plant material had risen to a fine art, and we are still very much influenced by the methods and styles of that period.

Now that gardening is among the most popular leisure activities and there is a renewed interest in Victorian and Edwardian styles, everlasting plants are enjoying a revival that may be even more widespread than their original popularity. Flower arranging is no longer the exclusive domain of the lady of leisure. Men and women of various ages and interests are growing, buying, preserving, and arranging everlasting flowers.

This book is for all of them. It is an encyclopaedia of plant varieties suitable for preservation, botanical and horticultural information, as well as suggestions for using everlastings in arrangements.

Its purpose is to broaden the horizons and enrich the resources of anyone who enjoys flowers. It encourages readers to see the potential for beautiful everlastings everywhere—to notice blossoming weeds on the roadsides and vacant lots, to see common grasses in a new way, and even to consider the produce in the grocery store with a new eye. May the joy we take in this be everlasting as well.

METHODS OF PLANT PRESERVATION

AIR-DRYING

The simplest of all methods, air-drying allows plant material to dehydrate naturally. Plants respond well to this method soon after they are picked. The foliage of most flowers does not respond well to air-drying, however, and should therefore be removed.

Air-drying may be as easy as standing the stems in a dry vase or basket until they are dry. In this way, plants develop life-like curves. Materials that respond well to this method include grasses—members of the *Gramineae* family, including bamboos—and many shrubs. Some plants, like Oriental bittersweet and heathers, dry best in an arrangement.

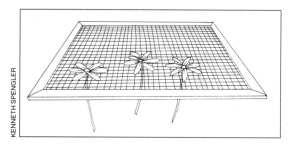

Flowers that would droop on their stems if they were dried upright are tied into loose bundles and hung upside down, tightly secured with a string or rubberband. They can be hung from hooks or rods. Alternatively, chicken wire can be attached to the ceiling of your drying area and used as a surface from which to suspend the material with the stems hanging through the holes. The room or area in which you air-dry plants should be dark and well ventilated.

WATERING

Sometimes a flower or leaf needs to dry slowly to preserve its color or shape, so it is placed in a vase or other container in about 2 inches (5 centimeters) of water. As the water evaporates, the stems absorb a little of the moisture, which slows the drying process. Be sure that all stems reach the bottom of the container. For the method to work most effectively, cut stems at an angle, so that they receive optimal moisture. Some plants only require a week to dry; others need three weeks or more.

PRESSING

Nearly everyone has at some time saved a flower or a leaf by pressing it between the pages of a book. Pressed flowers are especially pretty in framed designs, while pressed leaves are effective both framed and in arrangements. Wooden flower presses capable of holding many layers of plants are available. These consist of wooden boards with holes drilled into the corners stacked on top of one another. Material is placed on absorbent paper between the boards, and then screws are tightened in the holes to form a sandwich. This method is quite effective for flowers that are difficult to press and can be constructed at home using two small plywood boards.

If you don't want to construct a wooden flower press, an old telephone directory is a good alternative. Arrange flower petals and leaves carefully as you close the

KENNETH SPENGLER

SAND

While sand is one of the most common and effective drying procedures, it is not the easiest. Choice and preparation of the sand is vital. By far the best for drying plants is the oolitic sand from the shores of Great Salt Lake in Utah. Instead of sharply fractured particles of stone, it is comprised of tiny, waterworn fragments of fine shell. Each grain is round, which avoids damage to tender petals, and the sand's chemical makeup helps to preserve natural colors. If you do not have the oolitic variety, a fine, clean beach sand may be used. Wash it thoroughly by stirring in large amounts of water. After washing, dry thoroughly by spreading in a thin layer.

To dry flowers, choose a container a little larger than the plant material

book to be sure they are spread apart from one another and not folded. It is often more effective to separate the leaves from the flowers and to allow all but a little bit of the stem to be pressed separately. Stems can be manipulated into graceful curves before the book is shut. Larger foliage and entire branches of leaves can be air-dried between sheets of newsprint. These heavier materials do not require tight pressing as delicate blossoms do; a light weight such as a piece of masonite or plywood will do. Papers should be porous and not have a shiny, coated surface.

Plants that come in shades of orange and yellow—such as the African daisy, coral bells, bleeding heart, dill and viola—are among the best to press. Greens that respond well to pressing include leaves of maple, beech, dusty miller, ferns, hosta, and palm. Pressing requires about two weeks' time.

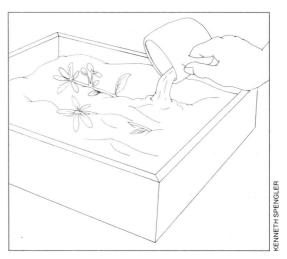

KENNETH SPENGLER

and begin with a 1-inch (2.5-centimeter) base of dry sand. Place the flower or flowers on it, and slowly dribble a stream of dry sand over the plant material to fill all the crevices and support its outer sides. The object is to cover the plant completely without changing its shape. Sometimes it is helpful to use a little funnel made of a rolled cone of paper to distribute sand evenly in exactly the right places. Do not cover the container. Check on the flower after three weeks.

SILICA GEL

A commercial product, silica gel is quite expensive, so it should be used as judiciously as possible. It produces stunning results, preserving much of the original color of flowers. Use a container as close to the plant size and shape as you can find, and make sure that it can be sealed tightly. Silica gel will absorb moisture from the air just as readily as from the plants, so a tight seal is important for quick drying. Follow the same procedure as for drying with sand. Since it takes only a few days to completely dry flowers, silica gel can be reused quickly. When the little blue crystals turn pink, it has absorbed all the moisture it can hold and needs to be baked slowly in an oven on the lowest setting, spread in a thin layer, until the crystals turn blue again. Be sure to cool the silica gel before using. Since this dessicant works quickly, it is especially well suited to fragile plants and those of delicate colors.

METHODS AND TOOLS FOR ARRANGING

Entire books are devoted to the subject of arranging everlastings, and there are as many styles of dried arrangements as there are designs for fresh bouquets. In order to use your everlastings to best advantage, there are a number of tools and materials that you may need.

Some plants require *straight wire* to reinforce or lengthen their stems. Choose 28-to-30-gauge wires for these purposes and have a *wire cutter* on hand to cut wire to the appropriate length for each plant. *Floral tape* (*gutta percha*) is also useful in sealing joints between wires and stems and for camouflaging wire. It is available in a variety of colors, so choose one that complements your design.

You have a number of choices for securing materials so that they stay in place in your arrangement. *Styrofoam* is the most commonly used base for arrangements and works best with thick stems and branches because it is quite dense. Double-sided tape will keep Styrofoam in place and short-stemmed foliage will hide the mechanics of the design. Styrofoam can be reused.

Brown foam and *Sahara* are available in neutral colors that make for a better aesthetic presentation than Styrofoam if the base will show. Because they are more porous, they also offer more flexibility than Styrofoam, but are more expensive. Glue must be used to hold these materials in place. They should not be reused.

Moist foams, such as Bar-Fast, are also available. These actually dry around stems, securely locking them in place. Such foams are usually more expensive than other methods, but are very easy to use; however, they cannot be reused.

The *Japanese pinholder*, often used with ikebana arrangements, is another arranging option. To use these insert stems and small branches between the pins. While difficult for the beginner to work with, pinholders offer more advanced students of floral design greater flexibility. The resulting arrangements are unencumbered by vases.

Other materials to have on hand are soft bristle brushes, oil paints, and fabric dyes. Very small amounts of oil paint can be used to restore the color in the center of a flower. To dye the sturdier dried plant material, use standard fabric dyes. Some natural materials, such as buckthorn and cattails, benefit from a coating of spray *varnish*, which not only gives them sheen, but also a protective coating. To protect without gloss, use a floral fixative spray.

GARDEN ZONE MAP

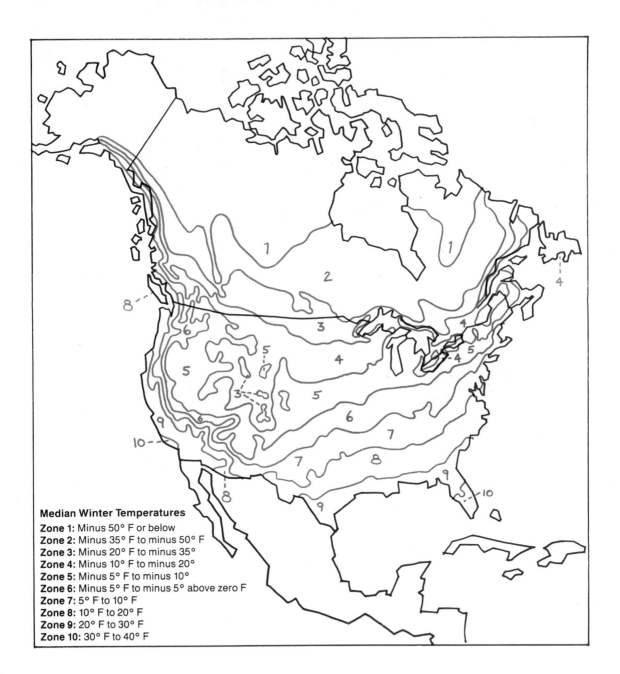

Median Winter Temperatures
Zone 1: Minus 50° F or below
Zone 2: Minus 35° F to minus 50° F
Zone 3: Minus 20° F to minus 35°
Zone 4: Minus 10° F to minus 20°
Zone 5: Minus 5° F to minus 10°
Zone 6: Minus 5° F to minus 5° above zero F
Zone 7: 5° F to 10° F
Zone 8: 10° F to 20° F
Zone 9: 20° F to 30° F
Zone 10: 30° F to 40° F

A DIAGRAM OF A FLOWER

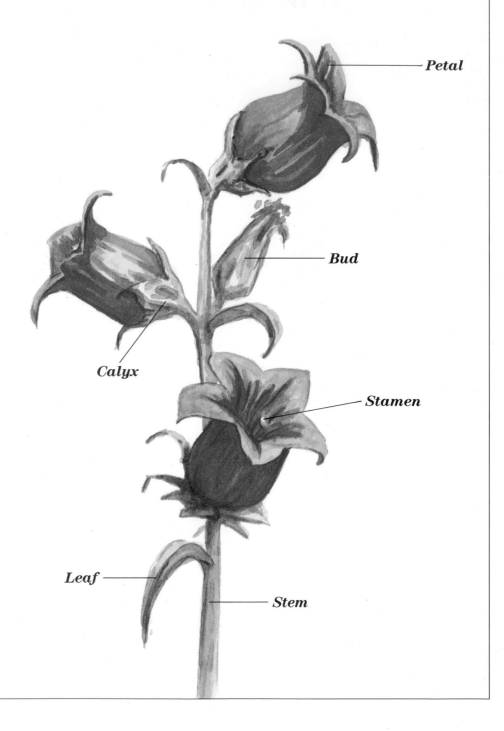

Petal

Bud

Calyx

Stamen

Leaf

Stem

KENNETH SPENGLER

THE ENCYCLOPAEDIA OF EVERLASTINGS IN ALPHABETICAL ORDER BY BOTANICAL NAME

Genus/species: Abelmoschus
 esculentus
Common name: okra
Annual
Region: native to West Africa;
 common crop in southern U.S.
Color: green pods dry to brown
Height: 3 to 5 feet (90 to 150
 centimeters)
Arrangement: woodsy, wild, or
 modern styles

Although associated with the U.S. South, okra may be grown in northern gardens if it is started indoors. It is also found in grocery stores. Its long, ribbed pods should be picked before they mature on the vine, or the plant will stop producing. Air-dry the pods by laying them on a screen or rack, where they will often take on interesting curves. Wire them to stems to use individually. Most okra matures to shades of tan, but the Gurney Seed Company offers a red okra that is not only attractive in the garden but dries to a rich black. Okra pods may also be bleached to a creamy white; they are often found in this color at floral suppliers.

KENNETH SPENGLER

MARY CLOSE

Genus/species: *Acacia armata, A. decurrens,* var.
Common name: mimosa
Tree
Region: grown in semitropical zones
Color: yellow
Height: 20 to 30 feet (6 to 9 meters)
Arrangement: long, sweeping lines best for large and exotic arrangements

The fragrant puffs of *Acacia* are familiar to arrangers of fresh flowers and are usually available from florists. Both the flowers and foliage can be air-dried hanging or, for more graceful curves, allowed to stand in a vase of water until they have dried. The foliage can also be dried alone.

Genus/species: *Acanthus mollis*
Common name: bear's breech, artist's acanthus
Perennial
Region: native to Mediterranean; grown in garden zones 8 through 10
Color: white and mauve blossoms
Height: 2 to 4 feet (60 to 120 centimeters)
Arrangement: leaves or seedheads attractive as background in large arrangements

Acanthus leaves were carved into history as the inspiration for the design of the capitals on ancient Greek columns. Their graceful, deeply sculptured lines make them favorites for large arrangements. The leaves can be air-dried by hanging or pressing lightly between papers. The attractive seedheads form if the flowers are not picked.

KENNETH SPENGLER

Genus/species: *Acer saccharum*
Common name: sugar maple
Tree
Region: eastern North America
from Newfoundland south to
Georgia, and midcontinent from
Ontario south to Texas
Color: autumn leaves are red,
orange, and yellow
Height: 60 to 80 feet (18 to 24
meters)
Arrangement: showy color best in
large arrangements

The distinctive, broad, deeply cut
leaves of maples turn eastern U.S.
landscapes bright orange and red in
the fall. These colors soften a bit in
drying but remain surprisingly
bright. Press flat sprays between layers of soft paper, under a weight,
making sure that the leaves lie in a
single layer and do not overlap. Or
treat whole sprays in glycerin. The
Norway maple, a European native,
has yellow leaves in the fall and may
be treated in the same way as the
sugar maple. The winged seeds of the
maples, if picked in clusters before
they fall, are attractive as accents for
arrangements or wreaths.

WILLIAM S. MOYE

ANITA MARCI

Genus/species: *Achillea millefolium, A. filipendulina*
Common name: yarrow, common yarrow, fern-leaf yarrow
Perennial
Region: grown in garden zones 3 through 10
Color: yellow, white, and pink
Height: 2 to 4 feet (60 to 120 centimeters)
Arrangement: large heads make a bold accent in any arrangement; attractive combined with field grasses in autumn bouquets or with purple delphinium (see page 74) for dramatic summer baskets; also good on large wreaths

The white yarrow that grows wild throughout North America may be dried, although its color is dull compared to the bright yellow garden varieties. Pink shades are beautiful in the garden, but they fail to hold their color as well as the long-lasting yellows. Dry all *Achilleae* by hanging them in an airy place. Pick them before they are quite at full bloom for the best results.

Genus/species: *Aconitum napellus*
Common name: monkshood
Perennial
Region: garden zones 3 through 8
Color: blue, purple, white, and yellow
Height: 2 to 3 feet (60 to 90 centimeters)
Arrangement: combines beautifully with stock, roses, and feathery foliage for a dramatic bouquet

Although monkshood is not an easy flower to dry successfully because it is fragile, it is well worth trying. Its tall spikes should be picked before fully bloomed and hung separately to air-dry. Sand or silica gel works well, but the large flower heads require a lot of dessicant to cover them.

KENNETH SPENGLER

Genus/species: *Agrimonia*
    eupatoria
Common name: agrimony
Perennial
Region: garden zones 3 through 8
Color: yellow blossoms; brown pods
Height: 2 to 3 feet (60 to 90
    centimeters)
Arrangement: spikes make a good
    accent or background in formal
    bouquets

Agrimony found its way into gardens as a dye plant, but its spikes of tiny yellow blossoms earned it a place in the herb garden even after it was no longer used for dyes. If allowed to remain unpicked, it will form a spike of firm brown seedpods, which are useful as accents or placed fan-like in the background of formal bouquets. It is also appropriate for wild harvest arrangements, swags, or wreaths.

WILLIAM S. MOYE

KENNETH SPENGLER

Genus/species: *Ajuga reptans*
Common name: carpet bugleweed, ajuga
Perennial
Region: common in North America and Europe
Color: purple; hybrids pink, red, and white
Height: 5 to 7 inches (13 to 18 centimeters)
Arrangement: flowers and leaves attractive in small arrangements

Ajuga has escaped from gardens in North America, where it was brought as a ground cover and rock garden plant. Its shiny oval leaves turn reddish brown in the fall and may be dried in sand or drying medium, along with the flower heads. These may be wired in bunches to longer stems for use in larger arrangements.

Genus/species: *Albizia julibrissin*
Common name: silk tree,
sometimes called mimosa because
of its similar appearance
Perennial shrub
Region: garden zones 5 through 10
Color: pink flowers; green pods
Height: 8 to 10 feet (2.4 to 3 meters)
Arrangement: pods are effective in
clusters, especially in softening
the effect of brightly colored
flowers

The seeds are visible in these long
green pods, which grow in clusters on
a mimosa-like tree. They are, as
might be assumed, a relative of the
acacia. The terminal clusters of pink
flowers are fragrant, making this a
good yard shrub. Pick the pods while
green and dry them in sand or silica
gel. They will require wiring if they
are to be used upright, but they also
are quite effective as hanging clusters at the edges of larger arrangements.

WILLIAM S. MOYE

WILLIAM S. MOYE

Genus/species: *Alchemilla mollis,*
A. vulgaris
Common name: lady's-mantle
Perennial
Region: garden zones 3 through 8
Color: yellow
Height: 6 to 12 inches (15 to 30
centimeters)
Arrangement: flowers good as
fillers; leaves favored as an accent
in English-country-style bouquets

Varieties of lady's-mantle grow
wild in eastern Canada and New England and have been herb garden favorites since Medieval days when
they were prized by alchemists
(hence the Latin genus name). The
clusters of tiny yellow blossoms
should be cut at the peak of bloom
and hung to air-dry. The deeply
pleated leaves can be dried in sand to
retain their depth or pressed flat
between layers of paper.

KENNETH SPENGLER

Genus/species: *Allium cepa,. A. viviparum*
Common name: Egyptian onion, top onion
Perennial
Region: native to Nile Valley, grown in temperate garden zones
Color: purple or reddish bulbs
Height: 3 to 4 feet (90 to 120 centimeters)
Arrangement: looks great as a part of kitchen wreaths or modern arrangements

Unlike other members of the onion family, these onions develop clusters of bulbs at the top of their stems. The clusters can be air-dried, then wired for use. They are a favorite for kitchen wreaths because the tiny bulbs can be snipped off and used in place of shallots or onions in cooking. Allow plenty of room in the garden, since these can be sprawling and rather ungainly.

Genus/species: *Allium schoenoprasum, A. tuberosum,* var.
Common name: chive, garlic chive, Oriental garlic, Chinese chive
Perennial
Region: garden zones 3 through 10
Color: pink and white
Height: 1 to 2 feet (30 to 60 centimeters)
Arrangement: heads used primarily on herb wreaths

Like nearly all *Alliums*, the heads of chive dry well if picked when they first come into bloom. The Oriental variety also dries well on the plant, making an interesting light brown seedhead. Other ornamental *Alliums* may also be air-dried, although the larger ones are more fragile and do better in silica gel. The ornamental *Alliums* grow much taller than chives, often three to five feet (one to one-and-a-half meters). The stems of all *Alliums* are hollow, making them easy to mount on longer stems for arranging.

ANITA MARCI

Genus/species: *Althaea rosea* (syn. *Alcea rosea*)

Common name: hollyhock

Perennial

Region: native to China and the Balkans; grown in temperate garden zones

Color: white, yellow, pink, lavender, and red

Height: 5 to 9 feet (1.5 to 2.7 meters)

Arrangement: pretty in swags and wreaths

These dry very well in sand, and the calyx (see diagram, page 14) can be touched up with a little thinned green oil or acrylic paint. To dry the entire stalk of blossoms, hang it upside down in a large paper bag. These are properly classified as perennials, but they may be grown as annuals in zones nine and ten.

WILLIAM S. MOYE

ANITA MARCI

Genus/species: *Amaranthus caudatus, A. tricolor*

Common name: love-lies-bleeding, tampala

Annual

Region: native to the Far East; grown in temperate garden zones

Color: red to rich, electric green

Height: 2 to 5 feet (60 to 150 centimeters)

Arrangement: red varieties useful as accents; green attractive with *Achillea*, bittersweet, or orange strawflowers (see pages 18, 52, and 97)

The very look of this plant speaks of Victorian gardens and parlors. It is a tropical plant, so it should be planted early, indoors, for setting out in northern gardens. Pick the stalks when about half the blossoms are open and half are still tightly closed and hang them to dry. For curved shapes, allow them to dry in a vase with just a little water.

Genus/species: *Amaranthus cruentus, A. hypochondiracus*

Common name: prince's-feather, golden grain amaranth

Annual

Region: native of Mexico; grown in garden zones 6 through 10

Color: red-purple, gold, and green seedheads

Height: 6 feet (1.8 meters)

Arrangement: large, showy plumes add drama to large arrangements and make good filler in smaller ones if used with very short stems

Once a prized food of the peoples of Mexico, amaranth is once again being grown as a grain. It requires a long season of as much as 150 warm days to form the seedheads needed for both food and ornamental use. Leave these seedheads on the stalk only until they are fully formed and colored, then air-dry by hanging them or standing them upright in a dry container.

KENNETH SPENGLER

ANITA MARCI

Genus/species: *Anaphalis margaritacea*
Common name: pearly everlasting
Perennial
Region: native to Asia; grown in garden zones 3 through 6
Color: white
Height: 1 to 3 feet (30 to 90 centimeters)
Arrangement: attractive with any delicate flower; perfect for wreaths

Pearly everlasting is a common roadside wildflower in most of the U.S., but it is equally welcome in gardens for its silvery foliage and clusters of papery white flowers. Pick these flowers before the centers have fully opened or the blossoms will burst as they dry. Hang in bunches to air-dry. The stems may need reinforcing with wire for use in bouquets. Clusters of the flowers are used on herb wreaths, where they blend especially well with pink rosebuds (see page 151).

Genus/species: *Anemone pavonina, A. coronaria,* var.
Common name: windflower, anemone
Perennial
Region: garden zones 5 through 8
Color: pinks, blues, mauves, and reds
Height: 6 to 24 inches (15 to 60 centimeters)
Arrangement: delicate blossoms best in airy springtime bouquets with pink roses and gypsophila

Anemone should be started indoors in northern garden zones, but it will usually succeed as a perennial. It blooms prolifically. Dry the blossoms in sand or silica gel, face up. The larger blossoms will be more fragile and must be handled carefully, but their delicate appearance is the main source of their charm in dried bouquets.

MARY CLOSE

Genus/species: *Anethum*
graveolens
Common name: dill
Annual
Region: garden zones 3 through 10
Color: green
Height: 2 to 4 feet (60 to 120
centimeters)
Arrangement: soft, airy filler in
light styles

The umbrella-shaped clusters of dill seeds make a light foliage background for small carnations, pinks, and even pink roses. It is a nice alternative to *Gypsophila* (see page 96), providing a green background instead of white. Pick the stalks after the seeds have formed, but before they darken. Save a number of the hollow lower stems, since they are perfect as holders to lengthen short-stemmed flowers for arranging. Air-dry by standing them in a dry vase or by hanging.

WILLIAM S. MOYE

ROMAN SZOLKOWSKI

Genus/species: *Anigozanthos*
coccineus, A. flavidus, var.
Common name: kangaroo paw
Perennial
Region: native to Australia; grown
in Southern California
Color: yellow and purple
Height: 2 to 3 feet (60 to 90
centimeters)
Arrangement: the brilliant color
provides a good accent

Kangaroo paw is grown only in a small area of the U.S., but it is usually available at florist shops. It is best dried by standing the long stems in a vase with a little water and leaving them for about two weeks. The purple flowers will darken as they dry; the yellow will remain brilliant. Be careful in handling the dried flowers, since they become brittle and fragile.

WILLIAM S. MOYE

Genus/species: *Antennaria rosea*
Common name: pussytoe,
    cat's-paw
Perennial
Region: native to American West;
    grown in temperate garden zones
Color: pearly white to rose
Height: to 12 inches (30 centimeters)
Arrangement: use for filler or as
    the base material of tight
    arrangements with brighter colors
    as accents

Antennaria looks much like the pearly everlasting (*Anaphalis*) varieties (see page 26), and is used in the same ways. Pick just before the flowers reach full bloom and hang to air-dry. *Antennaria*'s light color takes well to dyeing, but be careful not to use too deep and artificial a shade. Dip the heads quickly into the dye and remove them to check the color. If it is not dark enough, repeat the quick dipping.

Genus/species: *Anthemis nobilis*
Common name: Roman chamomile,
    garden chamomile, Russian
    chamomile
Perennial
Region: garden zones 3 through 10
Color: white blossoms with yellow
    centers
Height: 12 to 14 inches (30 to 35
    centimeters)
Arrangement: good for miniature
    work or in clusters in larger
    arrangements, especially with
    pearly everlasting (see page 26)

These aromatic, daisy-like flowers are grown not only for use in arrangements, but also for potpourri and for the tea made famous in Beatrix Potter's *The Tales of Peter Rabbit*. Pick the flowers when they are just short of full bloom and air-dry them by hanging. If the white petals shrivel, simply trim them off and use the tidy yellow buttons that remain.

KENNETH SPENGLER

Genus/species: *Anthemis tinctoria*
Common name: golden marguerite, dyers marguerite
Perennial
Region: garden zones 3 through 10, except Gulf Coast
Color: yellow
Height: 2 to 3 feet (60 to 90 centimeters)
Arrangement: attractive in all styles

The daisy-like blossoms of the marguerite earned their place in early herb gardens as a dye plant, but their bright color and long blooming season have made them a choice for perennial borders as well. Pick the plants with long stems and hang to air-dry in small bunches. When the centers are entirely dry, carefully remove the petals to leave the yellow buttons. These may be used individually or wired into clusters.

WILLIAM S. MOYE

ROMAN SZOLKOWSKI

Genus/species: *Anthurium scherzeranum*
Common name: flamingo flower
Perennial
Region: native to South America and the West Indies
Color: red, pink, and orange
Height: 2 to 3 feet (60 to 90 centimeters)
Arrangement: used in modern and tropical arrangements

Anthurium always arrests the traveler's attention in tropical gardens, since it is so different from any temperate zone flower. They may be grown in more northerly areas as a houseplant and are sometimes found fresh in florist shops. To dry, cut the stem at a sharp angle and stand it in a vase with about two inches (five centimeters) of water until the flower is papery. They need to be handled carefully when dry.

Genus/species: *Antirrhinum majus*
Common name: snapdragon
Annual
Region: native to Mediterranean; now in gardens everywhere
Color: red, purple, yellow, and white
Height: varieties from 6 inches to 4 feet (15 to 120 centimeters)
Arrangement: various sizes add bright spikes of color to all styles

Snapdragons grow so easily from seed or nursery plants that they have become a favorite of gardeners everywhere. To get the maximum number of blossoms, pinch out the tips of plants when they are about four inches (ten centimeters) tall. Pick stems before all buds have opened and dry them on their sides in sand or silica gel. If flowers are allowed to mature on the plant and drop, striking spikes of seedheads will form. These may be used in wild arrangements or to add an accent to more formal ones.

ANITA MARCI

Genus/species: *Arctotis grandis*
Common name: African daisy
Annual
Region: native to South Africa;
  grown in temperate garden zones
Color: pearly white to pink; hybrids
  orange, red, and purple
Height: 15 to 24 inches (38 to 60
  centimeters)
Arrangement: both the flower and
  the gray-green foliage are almost
  universally useful in larger
  arrangements

The blossoms of the African daisy
(not to be confused with *Acrolynium*,
which is also called the African
daisy) are often as large as three
inches (eight centimeters) in diameter, making it one of the showier of
the dried flowers. Be sure to pick the
flowers early in the day, since like
strawflowers, they begin to close at
night. Air-dry by hanging each stem
separately to avoid crushing.

KENNETH SPENGLER

Genus/species: *Armeria maritima*
Common name: sea pink, thrift
Perennial
Region: native to the British coast;
  garden zones 4 through 9
Color: pink and white
Height: 12 to 18 inches (30 to 45
  centimeters)
Arrangement: pretty with ferns or
  artemisia (see page 32) and white
  flowers

A relative of statice (see page 113),
Armeria may still be found listed under its old classification of *Statice armeria*. It thrives on salt spray and is a
favorite for seaside gardens. It also
does well in rock gardens and is often
found in nurseries for this use. Hang
the stalks to air-dry.

ANITA MARCI

ANITA MARCI

Genus/species: *Artemisia albula*
Common name: artemisia, silver king artemisia, silver queen artemisia
Perennial
Region: garden zones 4 through 10, except Gulf Coast
Color: pale, silver-green leaves and flowers
Height: 2 to 4 feet (30 to 120 centimeters)
Arrangement: the mainstay of herb wreaths; also useful in all styles of dried bouquets for its full foliage and soft color

The flowers of these artemisiae are inconspicuous beads set in tall spires above the foliage. Pick artemisia as soon as these flowers are fully formed but before they have over-bloomed. Strip the lower darkened leaves, then dry the stalks by hanging or by standing them in a dry vase or basket. For wreath bases, curve the fresh stalks around wreath frames while they are still supple and wrap them lightly with wire to hold. These bases may be stored for later use or decorated while fresh.

Genus/species: *Asclepias syriaca,*
A. exaltata, A. physocarpa, var.
Common name: milkweed
Perennial
Region: grows wild throughout
North America
Color: pink, white, and mauve
blossoms; tan pods
Height: 2 to 4 feet (60 to 120
centimeters)
Arrangement: attractive in wild
and modern arrangements and in
cone wreaths

The pods of common milkweed are
more warty and coarse than those of
its relative, the butterfly weed (see
page 34), but they are attractive in
the right context. These are favored
less for arrangements and more for
wreaths and novelty uses. Milkweed
is used for wings on pinecone angels
and points on natural treetop stars, as
well as frames for tiny dried flower
arrangements. *A. physocarpa,* which
has pods the size of walnuts, is the
best for use in bouquets.

KENNETH SPENGLER

KENNETH SPENGLER

Genus/species: *Asclepias tuberosa*
Common name: butterfly weed
Perennial
Region: a common wildflower throughout most of North America; garden zones 4 through 10
Color: orange flowers; light brown pods
Height: 1 to 2 feet (30 to 60 centimeters)
Arrangement: pods are useful in wild bouquets or as accents in more formal work; good for a light touch in cone wreaths

Butterfly weed differs from its common milkweed cousins by its brilliant, flat-topped blossom clusters. Usually orange, it grows in varieties of scarlet, gold, and pink. All of these are beautiful as garden flowers, and they may be dried in silica gel, although the colors do fade somewhat. Of primary interest are the elegant, long, spindle-shaped seed pods. Gather these after the silky seeds disperse in the fall. They may be used as they grow, several to a branch, in modern or large wild arrangements, or separated and wired to stems for single use. Remember that these must be grown from seed; do not try to transplant them from the wild.

Genus/species: *Astilbe astilboides,*
    A. chinensis
Common name: astilbe
Perennial
Region: garden zones 4 through 8
Color: red, pink, purple, and white
Height: 2 to 3 feet (60 to 90
    centimeters)
Arrangement: a favorite in formal
    and fan-shaped arrangements for
    background

Astilbe is popular for shaded gardens, since it performs well without sun. Although its feathery plumes can be air-dried, they shrink considerably. For best results, dry the stalks, lying on their sides, in sand or silica gel.

MARY CLOSE

ANITA MARCI

Genus/species: *Astrantia major*
Common name: masterwort
Perennial
Region: native to England; garden
  zones 3 through 8
Color: silver to rose
Height: 2 to 3 feet (60 to 90
  centimeters)
Arrangement: used in small-scale
  arrangements and herb wreaths

The flowers of *Astrantia* are small,
which makes them best suited to miniature arrangements, but they may
be wired in clusters for use in larger
bouquets. Several are often combined on a florist's pick for use on
herb wreaths. Strip the leaves before
hanging these flowers to dry.

Genus/species: *Baccharis
  halimifolia*
Common name: baccharis,
  groundsel tree, sea myrtle,
  consumption weed
Perennial
Region: native to the East Coast of
  North America
Color: white
Height: 6 to 12 feet (1.8 to 3.6
  meters)
Arrangement: excellent filler in all
  styles of arrangement

Look for baccharis in coastal
marshes in the late autumn. Pick it
just as the white puffs begin to ap-
pear, since they shatter if the furry
pappus of the seed is left on the plant
too long. The stems are sturdy, so
these may be dried by standing upright in a basket or dry vase.

ANITA MARCI

Genus/species: *Banksia occidentalis, B. menziesii,* var.
Common name: Australian honeysuckle
Perennial shrub
Region: native to Australia; grown in garden zones 9 and 10
Color: maroon, red, orange, yellow, white, lilac, and brown
Height: from 2 feet (60 centimeters)
Arrangement: large flowers make dramatic accents in larger pieces

The thistle-like blooms of *Banksia* vary from nearly round to long cattail shapes, but they are always large and showy. The stems are firm, and the leaves of all varieties dry well around the heads, creating a nice frame for the flower as well as providing foliage in an arrangement. Air-dry all varieties by hanging or standing. Air-dry clusters of leaves for use alone.

KENNETH SPENGLER

ANITA MARCI

Genus/species: *Baptisia australis*
Common name: false indigo
Perennial
Region: garden zones 3 through 9
Color: blue when fresh; brown
when dried
Height: 3 to 5 feet (90 to 150
centimeters)
Arrangement: pods dramatic in
entire sprays for larger
arrangements; side shoots useful
in smaller ones

Baptisia is a favorite of gardeners
for its compact shape and blue, lu-
pine-like flowers. These produce
clusters of pods that turn very dark
as they ripen. Let them dry on the
plant or cut them when they are fully
formed and stand to dry. Some arrangers like to varnish the pods for a
high gloss and deepened color. The
blue-gray foliage may be preserved in
glycerin when it is at its peak.

Genus/species: *Bellis perennis*
Common name: English daisy
Annual and perennial
Region: native to England; now grows wild in most regions of North America
Color: pink, red, or white, with yellow center
Height: 6 inches (15 centimeters)
Arrangement: pretty in small arrangements

These delicate, single white or pink-rayed blossoms are the "Day's Eye" of English literature. They bloom in spring and summer and are grown as annuals in garden zones eight through ten and as perennials in garden zones three through seven. Pick before the petals are fully open, then dry in sand or silica gel with enough stem for wiring. The centers may be used alone by hanging the flowers to air-dry and removing the petals after they dry.

WILLIAM S. MOYE

Genus/species: *Bouteloua curtipendula*
Common name: side oats gramma (or gama)
Perennial
Region: native to the U.S. western ranges
Color: reddish tan stalks; orange and purple flowers
Height: 18 to 24 inches (45 to 60 centimeters)
Arrangement: a striking grass for all styles of arrangements

Side oats gramma is taller and coarser than blue gramma and its seeds are borne in two parallel rows on one side of the stalk where they dangle gracefully. It grows particularly well in very dry soils where others will not survive. Air-dry by hanging or standing.

WILLIAM S. MOYE

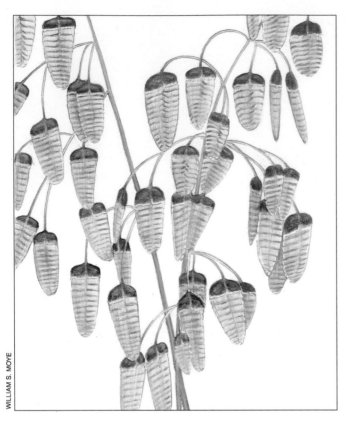

WILLIAM S. MOYE

Genus/species: Briza maxima, B. minor, B. minima
Common name: quaking grass
Annual
Region: garden zones 3 through 10
Color: tan, also red, brown, and bronzed green
Height: 9 to 24 inches (23 to 60 centimeters), depending on variety
Arrangement: adds interest and motion to any style

These flat, evenly shaped, oval seed clusters droop gracefully on slender, arched stems that branch from a main stalk. They are fragile and tremble at the slightest breeze or touch. They should be cut before the seeds are fully ripe, then dried by hanging or standing in a dry vase. They take very well to dyes.

Genus/species: Caesalpinia bonduc
Common name: kakalaioa, Hawaiian marble
Perennial
Region: native to South America; grown on Hawaiian volcanic slopes
Color: yellow flowers; tan pods
Height: climbs to height of support
Arrangement: useful in modern or wild arrangements and on cone wreaths

The spiny vines of kakalaioa grow over rocks and trees, with clusters of yellow flowers that turn into prickly, burr-like pods. Each about two inches (five centimeters) long, they split as they dry to reveal round, gray seeds about the size of marbles. These are used locally for necklaces and seed leis. Pick pods before or after they split, and wire them in clusters to longer stems for arrangements. They are easily wired onto cone wreaths as well.

WILLIAM S. MOYE

Genus/species: *Calendula officinalis*
Common name: pot marigold
Annual
Region: native to Mediterranean; grown in temperate zones
Color: bright orange-yellow
Height: 12 inches (30 centimeters)
Arrangement: showy and bright, good for grouping or use as a colorful accent

Pot marigolds are easy to grow from seed or as small plants purchased from the nursery, and they bear flowers all season. They are best dried in sand or silica gel and may need wiring to longer stems. If the silky petals seem loose, dribble a little glue into the center. Imperfectly dried blossoms may be saved for potpourri.

KENNETH SPENGLER

Genus/species: *Callistemon citrinus*

Common name: bottlebrush

Half-hardy shrub

Region: native to Australia and the U.S. Midwest; grown in garden zones 7 through 10

Color: red

Height: 3 to 6 feet (90 to 180 centimeters)

Arrangement: used as a focal point, especially with greens; attractive combined with purple delphinium (see page 74) and pale green grasses

Bottlebrush provides not only a good, bright red, but an attractive texture in arrangements as well. The plant may be grown potted in colder climates and the blooms air-dried by hanging singly. Its slightly lemon-scented leaves cling close to the stems and may be left on for drying. The dried flowers are also usually available from florists.

Genus/species: *Calluna vulgaris*
Common name: heather
Perennial
Region: native to Europe; grown in garden zones 4 through 8, except in arid areas
Color: pink, white, and red
Height: 18 inches (45 centimeters)
Arrangement: with or without flowers, an excellent filler in closely packed arrangements

Easily confused with its relative, spring heath, heather blooms only in the late summer. The evergreen foliage dries just as well as the blooming plant, by simply hanging it in bunches. To use heather as a wreath base, a job it performs very well, shape it around the frame while it is still fresh and supple, wiring loosely to hold it in place. Heather needs acid soil, of poor quality, and plenty of moisture to succeed in the garden.

ANITA MARCI

KENNETH SPENGLER

Genus/species: *Campanula medium*
Common name: Canterbury bell, bellflower
Annual, biennial, and perennial
Region: garden zones 3 through 10
Color: whites, pinks, and blues
Height: 18 to 36 inches (45 to 90 centimeters)
Arrangement: pretty with anemone (see page 26) in delicate spring arrangements

Grown as annuals in zones three through five, Canterbury bells are perennials and biennials in warmer regions. Dry the individual bells separately, face up, in sand or silica gel. Glue on individual stems or return to the original stalk. Keep in mind that the whites and pinks dry best, although the blues hold their color for a few months before fading to white.

Genus/species: *Campsis radicans,*
C. grandiflora

Common name: trumpet vine,
Chinese trumpet vine, Chinese
trumpet creeper, Chinese trumpet
flower

Perennial

Region: garden zones 5 through 9

Color: red-orange flowers; brown
pods

Height: climbs to height of support

Arrangement: pods used in modern
arrangements or as an accent in
others

Trumpet vine is common throughout the U.S. South in the wild, and it
has been introduced as an ornamental as far north as New England. Its
flowers are showy and attractive to
hummingbirds. The long, thin seed
capsules split and curve gracefully
and should be allowed to dry on the
vine. They can be used singly or
wired to stems in clusters.

KENNETH SPENGLER

Genus/species: *Canna flaccida, C. generalis*
Common name: Indian shot
Perennial
Region: native to West Indies; now grows wild in Gulf states
Color: yellow, orange, and red
Height: 3 to 5 feet (90 to 150 centimeters)
Arrangement: leaves best in modern arrangements; flowers good in any large arrangement

While these showy plants are usually dried for the dramatic leaves, the flowers, too, can be preserved. Cut individual blossoms from the stalk and brush them with powdered chalk before drying face up in sand. The strong, bold leaves can be dried by pressing lightly, or they may be rolled lengthwise around absorbent paper to dry in a tube shape.

Genus/species: *Capsella bursa-pastoris*
Common name: shepherd's purse
Annual
Region: native to Europe; grows wild throughout North America
Color: green to brown
Height: 6 to 18 inches (15 to 45 centimeters)
Arrangement: adds an airy, feathery quality to any style

Common in both untended areas and cultivated gardens around North America, shepherd's purse seed capsules come in a variety of shapes. Yet they are always flat and stand out from the central stem on little branches. They may be field dried or picked when green to air-dry by hanging or standing in a dry vase. Although this plant's overall effect is feathery, the stems are firm enough to help support weaker plant material in an arrangement.

WILLIAM S. MOYE

Genus/species: *Capsicum frutescens, C.* var.

Common name: pepper, red cayenne pepper, tabasco pepper, Hungarian wax pepper, cherry pepper

Annual

Region: native to South and Central America; grown in temperate garden zones

Color: red, green, yellow, and orange

Height: 2 to 3 feet (60 to 90 centimeters)

Arrangement: Used in kitchen wreaths and braided into bright ropes

Peppers need a long growing season to produce, but this can be easily solved in northern zones by planting them in black plastic mulch (a sheet of plastic covering the ground around the plants) and providing row covers in the fall for frost protection. The peppers may be dried by picking and hanging the entire plant, but more peppers are obtained by picking each pod as it ripens and laying it on a screen in a shady, airy place to dry. Or they may be strung by running a needle and stout thread through the stems. The fruit will shrivel but remain attractive and strong colored. They may be wired to stems for arrangements.

ANITA MARCI

WILLIAM S. MOYE

Genus/species: *Cardiospermum halicacabum*
Common name: balloon vine
Annual and perennial
Region: native to tropics; garden zones 9 and 10
Color: white flowers; green and brown pods
Height: climbs to height of support
Arrangement: brown seedpods most effective in harvest bouquets; green seedpods attractive in nearly any style of arrangement

Clusters of balloon-shaped seedpods follow tiny white flowers on these fast-growing vines. Although they are perennial in their native habitat, they sometimes perform well as annuals in northern garden zones. Their fast-growing stems are not very strong and need the support of a fence or trellis. Air-dry the pods to achieve light brown shades or dry them in silica gel or sand for a green result.

Genus/species: *Carlina acanthifolia, C. acaulis*
Common name: carlina, stemless thistle
Perennial
Region: native to Europe; grown in garden zones 4 through 8
Color: metallic gold, and white to reddish
Height: 12 to 24 inches (30 to 60 centimeters)
Arrangement: very versatile as a dramatic accent; combined with *Lunaria*, white strawflowers, and *Gypsophila* (see pages 118, 97, and 96) makes an elegant silver-white arrangement

The heads of *C. acanthifolia* grow up to five inches (thirteen centimeters) in diameter, while *C. acaulis* may be as large as twelve inches (thirty centimeters). There is only one flower per plant. Pick these summer blooms at their peak and hang them to dry separately. Although they take up quite a bit of garden space for a single flower yield, *Carlina* is such an interesting and dramatic flower, that it is worthwhile growing at least a few specimens.

KENNETH SPENGLER

ANITA MARCI

Genus/species: *Carthamus tinctorius*
Common name: safflower
Annual
Region: garden zones 3 through 10, but best in dry climates
Color: deep yellow and orange
Height: 2 to 3 feet (60 to 90 centimeters)
Arrangement: provides a colorful accent in any style arrangement

Safflower is a handsome addition to the herb garden, where it is known as a dye plant. Pick it when some flowers are open and some still in bud form, leaving the clusters of leaves near the blossoms and hanging the stems to dry. Or pick individual blossoms as they bloom and wire them to longer stems when dry.

Genus/species: *Cassia marilandica*
Common name: wild senna, cassia
Perennial
Region: garden zones 4 through 10
Color: yellow clusters; brown pods
Height: 4 to 7 feet (1.2 to 2.1 meters)
Arrangement: used in fairly large arrangements

The pods form after the yellow flowers drop. About four inches (ten centimeters) long, these may be dried right in the garden, where the fern-like foliage remains attractive. Pods can be used right on their zigzag stems in some arrangements, but they will have to be wired in more traditional ones.

WILLIAM S. MOYE

Genus/species: *Catalpa speciosa*
Common name: catalpa, western catalpa, Indian-bean, cigar tree, catawba
Ornamental tree
Region: native to Gulf Coast; grows in other garden zones
Color: white spring blossoms; brown pods
Height: 100 to 125 feet (30 to 38 meters)
Arrangement: blossoms are lovely combined with ferns; pods good in modern arrangements

These orchid-like flowers should be picked and dried separately in sand. The slender pods can be dried right on the tree where they may split into graceful curving halves or dry whole and straight. They are from ten to twenty inches (twenty-five to fifty centimeters) long and turn a very dark brown that creates a striking accent in arrangements.

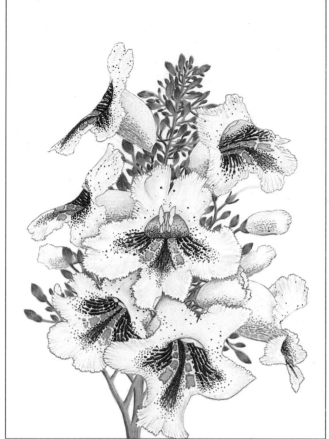

WILLIAM S. MOYE

ANITA MARCI

Genus/species: *Catananche caerulea*
Common name: Cupid's-dart
Annual and perennial
Region: native to Europe; garden zones 3 through 9
Color: blue
Height: 2 feet (60 centimeters)
Arrangement: silver bracts attractive with brighter colors; useful in place of cornflowers in delicate spring bouquets

In northern zones, Cupid's-dart should be started indoors and grown as an annual, but in warmer climates it may persist from year to year as it does in its native southern Europe. Collect bracts after the petals have faded, or pick the flowers just short of full bloom and dry them in sand or silica gel.

ANITA MARCI

Genus/species: *Celastrus orbiculatus, C. scandens*
Common name: Oriental bittersweet, American bittersweet
Perennial vine
Region: native to eastern North America
Color: orange
Height: climbs to 20 feet (6 meters), *orbiculatus* to 36 feet (11 meters)
Arrangement: used with greens, especially at Christmas; also good on vine wreaths

American bittersweet, *C. scandens,* bears fruit only at the tips of the twigs, making it more useful in arrangements than the Oriental variety, which bears fruit in small lateral clusters along the stems. Bittersweet is best picked after the leaves have dropped, but before the orange outer shells have opened. If they are picked before the leaves fall, these will have to be removed by hand; if picked after the shells open, the berries will drop as they dry. It is best to arrange bittersweet soon after it is cut to avoid handling after it is dry. Don't allow a bittersweet vine to twine around a living tree or shrub, since it will strangle it. Oriental bittersweet can be grown south of zone four.

Genus/species: *Celosia argentea cristata*
Common name: cockscomb
Annual
Region: native to Asia; grown in temperate garden zones
Color: orange, red, and purple
Height: 1 to 3 feet (30 to 90 centimeters)
Arrangement: useful, usually broken into smaller pieces, as a vivid color accent in dramatic arrangements

The large (up to ten inches, or twenty-five centimeters), convoluted, velvety heads of cockscomb are a great favorite of some gardeners and shunned as unbearably ugly by others. Pick them at the peak of bloom and air-dry by hanging the heads singly. Small sections may be broken off and wired to stems for a less overwhelming effect where touches of intense color are needed.

KENNETH SPENGLER

Genus/species: *Celosia argentea plumosa*
Common name: plume celosia, sometimes called feathered amaranth
Annual
Region: native to Asian tropics; grown in temperate garden zones
Color: orange, red, yellow, and gold
Height: 8 to 30 inches (20 to 76 centimeters)
Arrangement: especially useful in full autumn bouquets and swags because of its color and feathery, spiky shape

Plume celosia thrives best in hot climates and should be started indoors in the north. Cut spikes at their peak and hang them to dry in the dark. Their bright colors will mellow a bit. The feathery spikes may be used whole, or side shoots may be broken off and wired in clusters, leaving the center spike to be used in heavier arrangements.

KENNETH SPENGLER

KENNETH SPENGLER

Genus/species: *Centaurea cyanus*
Common name: bachelor's button,
  cornflower
Annual
Region: European native;
  naturalized throughout the U.S.
Color: blue, purple, pink, and
  magenta
Height: 1 to 2 feet (30 to 60
  centimeters)
Arrangement: attractive combined
  with tiny red roses, larkspur, and
  Lunaria, with *Gypsophila* as a
  filler (see pages 151, 63, 118, and
  96)

Bachelor's button, called cornflower in Europe, is the national
flower of Germany. Although it will
grow throughout the U.S., it performs best in the northern half. Pick
the flowers just short of full bloom
and dry them in sand or silica gel.
Since the stems are weak, the bract
may be wired before drying to support the flower later. Use them in delicate spring arrangements as focal
points.

Genus/species: *Centaurea moschata*
Common name: sweet sultan
Annual
Region: garden zones 3 through 10
Color: bright yellow
Height: 16 to 24 inches (40 to 60 centimeters)
Arrangement: yellow puffs good as accents in wild grass bouquets or with darker flowers and foliage

Northern gardeners will need to start these plants indoors for transplanting after the danger of frost is past. They are attractive in the garden and should be picked just before they reach full bloom. Dry the blooms in sand or silica gel or by hanging.

KENNETH SPENGLER

Genus/species: Centaurea rutifolia
(syn. *S. cineraria), C.*
gymnocarpa
Common name: dusty miller
Annual and perennial
Region: garden zones 3 through 10
Color: gray foliage
Height: 1 to 2 feet (30 to 60
centimeters)
Arrangement: foliage good in
Edwardian arrangements and
wreaths, especially combined with
pink and magenta flowers

The name dusty miller is confusing
because it also used as a common
name for *Senecio cineraria* (see page
162). Both are used for their thick,
gray-green foliage, which is easily
dried by lightly pressing. It can also
be air-dried without pressing, but
when dried this way it will not keep
its shape as well. Leaves are very effective when combined with the
more feathery *Artemesia* (see page
32) in herbal wreaths. They are quite
sturdy when dry and make excellent
background sprays for Williamsburg-
style arrangements, as well as foliage
to frame pastel nosegays. They are
also used in pressed flower pictures.
This genus grows as a perennial in
zones nine and ten.

Genus/species: *Chamaedaphne calyculata*
Common name: leatherleaf
Perennial
Region: all colder regions of North America
Color: white flowers; brown seedheads
Height: 2 to 3 feet (60 to 90 centimeters)
Arrangement: sprays of leaves nice in nearly any arrangement

Leatherleaf is a bog plant whose roots are often found in water. It retains its leaves all winter and can be gathered more easily when the spongy ground is frozen solid. In the fall, seed spikes form with small brown clusters along the stems on short twigs. The small cups split open at the seams to drop the seeds. The leaves, which can be air-dried by pressing in sprays or preserved in glycerin, look very much like those of the blueberry, to which this plant is closely related.

WILLIAM S. MOYE

KENNETH SPENGLER

Genus/species: *Chrysanthemum balsamita tanacetoides*
Common name: costmary, alecost, Bible leaf
Perennial
Region: garden zones 5 through 9
Color: green leaves; yellow blossoms
Height: 2 to 3 feet (60 to 90 centimeters)
Arrangement: leaves and flowers useful in all styles of arrangements

Late summer clusters of these small, compact yellow buttons can be air-dried by hanging. Left on the plant, they turn brown and remain firm for arrangements. Dry the leaves in clusters by pressing or hanging. Single pressed leaves were traditionally used as bookmarks in Bibles, hence the common name, Bible leaf. These leaves are very study. In northern zones the plant may not bloom until it has been established for several years.

ANITA MARCI

Genus/species: *Chrysanthemum maximum, C. leucanthemum*
Common name: Shasta daisy, oxeye daisy
Perennial
Region: garden zones 3 through 10
Color: white petals; yellow centers
Height: 1 to 3 feet (30 to 90 centimeters)
Arrangement: provides a fresh, informal touch to nearly any style

"Fresh as a daisy" is a common expression that does seem to describe the charm of this old-time favorite. *C. maximum*, the Shasta daisy found in gardens, is simply a bigger version of the wild oxeye daisy. Since the stems of each tend to be spindly when dry, it is a good idea either to wire them or to insert a pin in the base before drying in sand or silica gel. A light dusting of white powdered chalk on the petals before drying helps to keep them from becoming transparent. Shastas are also available in yellows, oranges, and other autumn colors in most seed catalogs.

Genus/species: *Chrysanthemum morifolium*
Common name: florist's chrysanthemum, button poms
Annual and perennial
Region: garden zones 3 through 10
Color: yellow and cream
Height: 2 to 3 feet (60 to 90 centimeters)
Arrangement: clusters of buttons useful as fillers in large arrangements and as accents in smaller ones

Few groups of flowers cause so much confusion in classification as the many *Chrysanthemum* varieties loosely known as florist's chrysanthemums. These include enormous variation in color, size, shape, and style. They have been classified by the National Chrysanthemum Society into several classes, of which "Pompon" is only one. These are the best varieties for drying, and they are easily recognized by their tiny, closely packed petals, which look almost like the centers of daisies. They grow in clusters and air-dry easily by standing in a dry vase or by hanging. If they should begin to drop petals, reinforce them at the base with a drop or two of diluted glue.

ANITA MARCI

Genus/species: *Chrysanthemum parthenium*
Common name: feverfew
Perennial and hardy biennial
Region: garden zones 3 through 10; grown as an annual in far northern zones
Color: yellow centers; white petals
Height: 2 to 3 feet (60 to 90 centimeters)
Arrangement: used as an accent, especially in miniatures

Sometimes classified as *Pyrethrum parthenium*, feverfew is really a chrysanthemum. It is well known in the herb garden for its insect-repelling qualities, and it grows wild in many parts of the U.S. The tiny petals will not dry well, but they can be removed after the flower has been air-dried by hanging. The clusters of tiny buttons that remain resemble the flower's relative, Bible leaf, and can be used wherever touches of bright yellow are needed.

Genus/species: *Cichorium intybus*
Common name: chicory
Perennial
Region: native to Europe; now grows wild in North America
Color: blue, occasionally pink or white
Height: 3 to 5 feet (90 to 150 centimeters)
Arrangement: blossoms useful in delicate pieces; pods good for wreaths

Chicory was brought to North America by immigrants for its root, which was a highly prized coffee additive. Pick flowers in the morning and dry them individually in sand. Air-dry the stems and glue the flowers in place after drying. Flowers left to mature in the field will develop into seed pods that hug the stalk in groups of two or three. These are useful in arrangements and on wreaths.

WILLIAM S. MOYE

Genus/species: *Clarkia elegans, C. pulchella*

Common name: clarkia, Rocky Mountain garland

Annual

Region: native to U.S. West; thrives in mountains of the U.S. Northwest

Color: pink, rose, red, purple, and white

Height: 2 to 3 feet (60 to 90 centimeters)

Arrangement: tall spikes best in airy pastel bouquets and formal, fan-shaped Williamsburg styles

Named for the explorer William Clark of Lewis and Clark fame, *Clarkia* grows wild throughout the mountains of the American Northwest. Its spikes bloom from the bottom upward. The blossoms can be air-dried on screens individually as they bloom, or the entire spike can be dried when the bottom is in full bloom. Individual blossoms may also be dried in sand or silica gel.

KENNETH SPENGLER

KENNETH SPENGLER

Genus/species: *Coix lacryma-jobi*
Common name: Job's tears
Annual
Region: native to East Indies; grown in temperate garden zones
Color: white, gray, brown, and black seeds
Height: 2 to 6 feet (60 to 180 centimeters)
Arrangement: good in modern and harvest bouquets

Job's tears are the seeds used in the ubiquitous necklaces sold throughout Caribbean markets, for they take dyes very well. To string the seeds, pierce while they are still soft. To dry for arrangements, cut clusters on long stems before the seeds are too dry. Hang to dry for erect seeds, or stand in a dry vase for curved stems with hanging seeds. These may be grown in northern climates by starting seeds indoors.

Genus/species: *Consolida ambigua, C. regalis, C. orientalis*
Common name: larkspur
Annual
Region: native to southern Europe; grown in temperate garden zones
Color: blue, pink, and white
Height: 3 to 5 feet (90 to 150 centimeters)
Arrangement: combines well with *Lunaria* and bachelor's buttons or with *Dianthus* (see page 118, 54, 75, and 76)

Widely misnamed as annual delphinium (see page 74), the larkspur is a separate genus. Larkspur air-dries well, either hanging or standing, if picked when about half of the florets are fully opened. It may also be dried in silica gel or sand, lying on its side. Larkspur is a favorite of arrangers for English-country-style bouquets, because of its soft colors and tall spikes. Like delphinium, it forms a spire of attractive seedheads if the flowers are left to mature on the plant.

KENNETH SPENGLER

WILLIAM S. MOYE

Genus/species: *Convallaria majalis*
Common name: lily-of-the-valley
Perennial
Region: native to Europe; grown in garden zones 3 through 7
Color: white
Height: 8 to 10 inches (20 to 25 centimeters)
Arrangement: best for dainty, miniature, or bridal arrangements

It is no wonder that this lovely, fragrant little flower has been carried to gardens worldwide, since it grows easily and blooms early. The one-sided series of white bells droop from a curving stem, and they should be dried in sand lying on their sides. The wide, shiny leaves may be pressed lightly to dry. Their delicate nature make these a favorite in bridal arrangements, and they are often used fresh in brides' bouquets.

Genus/species: *Cordyline terminalis*
Common name: ti
Perennial
Region: native to Polynesia; naturalized in Hawaii
Color: deep green, red, and purple leaves
Height: 1 to 2 feet (30 to 60 centimeters)
Arrangement: leaves add a dramatic touch, especially to modern and tropical arrangements

The ti is a lily brought to Hawaii by early Polynesians and quickly naturalized there. The traditional grass skirts are made from ti leaves, and they are also woven into sandals and nets. In ancient lore they are a symbol of divine power. Dry the leaves by pressing lightly. They are usually available at florist shops.

KENNETH SPENGLER

Genus/species: *Coreopsis grandiflora*
Common name: coreopsis
Hardy annual and perennial
Region: native to California; grown in garden zones 4 through 10
Color: yellow and gold, some with red centers
Height: 1 to 3 feet (30 to 90 centimeters)
Arrangement: a favorite in Victorian-style arrangements

This daisy-like flower lasts better if dusted lightly with powdered yellow chalk before drying face up in sand. It is a favorite garden flower used by fresh flower arrangers as well.

KENNETH SPENGLER

WILLIAM S. MOYE

Genus/species: *Cornus florida*
Common name: flowering dogwood
Ornamental tree
Region: U.S. South; grows as far
  north as coastal New England
Color: white blossoms, occasionally
  pink
Height: 10 to 30 feet (3 to 9 meters)
Arrangement: Oriental- and
  Williamsburg-style arrangements

Dogwood prefers woodland margins or the understory (lower layers) of open forests. Pick early in the spring, before the green centers open, choosing some while they still have the green tinge of immaturity. Dry in sand or silica gel. Since the tiny stems are hard to wire, try inserting a pin into the base before drying. Air-dry the branches and pin or glue the blossoms in place when they have dried. Gather sprays of the leaves while they are green or after they have turned red and press in newspapers, taking care not to overlap leaves. Leaves can also be preserved in glycerin. Another variety of dogwood, *C. nuttallii*, grows along the Pacific Coast and, although it lacks the distinctive dogwood shape, it dries just as well.

Genus/species: *Cortaderia*
   argentea
Common name: pampas grass
Perennial
Region: native to Argentina; grown
   in most mild temperate garden
   zones
Color: silvery white to pink
Height: 8 to 10 feet (2.4 to 3 meters)
Arrangement: plumes are most
   effective in large arrangements

This tall, handsome ornamental
grass may have single plumes as long
as three feet (one meter). It is just as
dramatic in the garden as it is in bold
arrangements. Pick it in late summer
or fall before it has become saturated
by rains. Although all plants flower,
female plants have the largest
plumes.

KENNETH SPENGLER

WILLIAM S. MOYE

Genus/species: *Cosmos bipinnatus*
Common name: cosmos
Annual
Region: native to Mexico; grown in temperate garden zones
Color: pink blossoms with yellow centers
Height: 3 to 6 feet (90 to 180 centimeters)
Arrangement: good accent when combined with paler pinks and whites in spring bouquets

These large, showy pink flowers are shaped like daisies. They are drought resistant and need a long summer growing season, so northern gardeners will want to start them indoors. They do especially well in gardens of the American Southwest. Pick cosmos just at full bloom and dry face down in sand for about two weeks.

Genus/species: *Crotalaria retusa*
Common name: rattlebox,
  sometimes called yellow sweet pea
Annual
Region: native to Asia; grown in
  garden zones 3 through 10
Color: Yellow flowers; brown
  seedpods
Height: 18 to 24 inches (45 to 60
  centimeters)
Arrangement: flowers useful in
  large arrangements with deep
  green foliage; pods good as accents
  in all settings

Although barely related, *Crotalaria* strongly resembles the sweet pea. The flower spikes should be picked when about three-fourths bloomed and dried horizontally in sand. Or allow flowers to mature and form seedpods, which can be air-dried by hanging individually.

ROMAN SZOLKOWSKI

Genus/species: *Cynara cardunculus, C. scolymus*
Common name: cardoon, artichoke
Perennial
Region: garden zones 8 through 10
Color: lavender, purple, and pink
Height: up to 5 feet (1.5 meters)
Arrangement: best in large, modern arrangements because of their imposing size

Both the cardoon and the common vegetable artichoke develop dramatic dried flower heads if allowed to ripen on the vine. The foliage becomes either silvery-gray or brown and holds a thistle-like flower. Dry the blooms on long stems by placing them in a vase with about two inches (five centimeters) of water for two months or longer. Supermarket artichokes, especially the small ones, may be dried by inserting heavy wire into the stem end and hanging. While these do not develop flowers, they are interesting additions to modern arrangements.

Genus/species: *Cyperus papyrus*
Common name: papyrus
Perennial
Region: native to Egypt and
   southern Europe; grown in garden
   zone 9
Color: green
Height: 6 to 8 feet (1.8 to 2.4 meters)
Arrangement: used in large
   arrangements; combines
   attractively with large, dramatic
   blossoms such as peony (see page
   137)

This aquatic sedge makes an out-
standing plant in greenhouse pools or
outdoors, as long as it is taken inside
in the winter in cooler areas. As a
potted plant it can easily grow to a
height of six feet (nearly two meters)
in a few years. It is usually available
dried from florists.

ROMAN SZOLKOWSKI

Genus/species: *Cytisus scoparius*
Common name: Scotch broom
Hardy shrub
Region: grown in garden zones 5
   through 10
Color: green leaves; yellow blossoms
Height: up to 8 feet (2.4 meters)
Arrangement: used for graceful
   outlines in larger arrangements;
   attractive combined with masses
   of pink roses (see page 151)

Broom is an easy shrub to grow in
mild climates, and it is readily available from florists. The narrow leaves
lie close to long, sweeping stems that
dry into graceful curves. It can be air-
dried either standing or hanging. It is
used most often for background foliage or to frame a modern arrangement, but shorter pieces can be used
effectively with more delicate
flowers.

ANITA MARCI

MARY CLOSE

Genus/species: *Dahlia pinnata, D. merckii*
Common name: dahlia
Annual and perennial
Region: hardy in garden zones 9 and 10
Color: red, yellow, orange, pink, and white
Height: 3 to 5 feet (90 to 150 centimeters); dwarf 1 to 2 feet (30 to 60 centimeters)
Arrangement: beautiful in full bouquets or combined with pure white flowers

Dahlias are popular even in those zones where they are grown as an annual. The tubers must be lifted in the fall and stored for spring planting, but the display of brilliant flowers amid deep green foliage is well worth the trouble. Pick them as they reach full bloom and dry them immediately in silica gel or sand. The stems tend to be weak, so it is best to wire them before drying.

Genus/species: *Datura stramonium*
Common name: jimsonweed
Annual
Region: native to southern, arid regions of North America; grown in garden zones 5 through 10
Color: white flowers; brown seedpods
Height: 30 inches (75 centimeters)
Arrangement: stalks good in large-scale arrangements; pods useful on cone or herb wreaths

Jimsonweed is now common in waste areas throughout southern and central North America. Strip the leaves before standing the stems upright to dry. All parts of the plant are poisonous.

ANITA MARCI

Genus/species: *Daucus carota*
Common name: Queen Anne's lace,
wild carrot
Biennial
Region: a European native; grows
wild throughout North America
Color: white
Height: 3 to 4 feet (90 to 120
centimeters)
Arrangement: creates a lacy setting
for *Rudbeckia* (see page 152) or
other bright, daisy-shaped flowers

Queen Anne's lace blooms throughout the summer and is a favorite
fresh flower in wild bouquets. It dries
easily in sand or borax, or it can be
air-dried by suspending it upright
with the stem down. A wide-mesh
screen is good for this method of drying. If the heads are allowed to remain on the plant after blooming,
they curl into interesting nest shapes
that are also useful in arrangements.

ANITA MARCI

MARY CLOSE

Genus/species: *Delphinium grandiflorum, D. elatum*
Common name: delphinium
Annual and perennial
Region: garden zones 3 through 10
Color: blue, purple, and white; occasionally pink, red, and yellow
Height: 18 to 48 inches (45 to 120 centimeters)
Arrangement: deep purple beautiful with yarrow (see page 18) for a dramatic summer bouquet; rich pinks combine well with *Limonium* and *Allium* (see pages 113 and 22)

Delphinium is one of the most useful dried flowers because it retains its rich blue shades and imposing size after drying. In southern zones (garden zones eight through ten) it is usually grown as an annual, but elsewhere its clumps grow steadily for many years. It may be dried standing in a dry vase, hanging, or in silica gel on its side. Individual florets may be removed as they bloom and dried by placing face down on a wire screen. Since each floret has a little stem attached, these may be wired singly to stems to use in smaller arrangements. The rich shades and more loosely packed florets of *D. grandiflorum* are the best for drying separately. Delphinium is at its best in grand-scale formal arrangements and combined with pinks and paler blues in summer garden bouquets. If the blooms are allowed to fade on the plant, they are followed by small seedheads, which are also attractive in arrangements.

Genus/species: *Dianthus alwoodii,
D. chinensis*
Common name: pink, gillyflower
Perennial
Region: garden zones 3 through 9
Color: white, cream, pink, apricot,
and red
Height: 6 to 15 inches (15 to 38
centimeters)
Arrangement: perfect in light, airy
spring bouquets

One of the favorite garden perennials, pinks were loved in Elizabethan England for their intense fragrance. Unfortunately, in an effort to improve their size and hardiness, the fragrance has been largely lost, and it is difficult to find the old, richly scented varieties in the U.S. Pick these flowers just short of full bloom, and dry them in sand or silica gel. They are also nice if picked as they are just opening from the bud stage. Secure the petals after the flower is dried with a drop of glue in the calyx if necessary.

KENNETH SPENGLER

KENNETH SPENGLER

Genus/species: *Dianthus barbatus*
Common name: sweet William
Perennial and biennial
Region: garden zones 4 through 10
Color: white, pink, and red
Height: 1 to 2 feet (30 to 60
centimeters)
Arrangement: dense clusters best
for accents, especially the brighter
pinks and reds

The flat-topped flower heads of sweet William are among the showiest of the spring garden flowers. Since they often grow with short stems, they may require wiring. Dry whole clusters face up in sand for about two weeks, and store them carefully to avoid crushing.

ROMAN SZOLKOWSKI

Genus/species: *Dianthus*
   caryophyllus
Common name: carnation
Annual and perennial
Region: garden zones 4 through 9
Color: red, pink, white, yellow, and
   apricot
Height: 10 to 24 inches (25 to 60
   centimeters)
Arrangement: useful in nearly any
   arrangement for their attractive
   color and form; lovely combined
   with ferns and small flowers

In choosing carnations to grow and
dry, it is best to stay with the miniature varieties. Not only are they easier to dry, but they bloom in great
profusion. One plant will provide
enough blossoms over its blooming
period to create an entire bouquet of
that color. North of zone six, start
them indoors early in spring and
grow them as annuals. They are perennial in zones six and seven and usually perform best as biennials farther
south. Dry them face up in sand or
silica gel. Drop a bit of quick-drying
glue into the calyx to hold the petals
in place and keep them from rattling.
The calyx of larger carnations or entire clusters of calyxes of the smaller
varieties make attractive green
"flowers" without the petals.

Genus/species: *Dicentra eximia, D. formosa, D. spectabilis*
Common name: bleeding heart
Perennial
Region: native to North America; grown in garden zones 4 through 10, except Gulf Coast
Color: deep pink blossoms, blue-green leaves
Height: 1 to 3 feet (30 to 90 centimeters)
Arrangement: arching stems look graceful in airy bouquets

One of the United States' most familiar spring garden flowers, bleeding heart presses beautifully, and it dries well in sand. Place the stems horizontally in a box, anchor the stem, and gently fill each heart with sand to hold it open. Cover the entire spray. The color will darken, but the shape will be perfectly preserved.

KENNETH SPENGLER

Genus/species: *Dicranopteris linearis*
Common name: uluhe, false staghorn fern, scrambling fan
Perennial
Region: native to Pacific islands and tropical Asia
Color: green fronds; reddish brown heads
Height: 10 to 15 feet (3 to 4.5 meters)
Arrangement: graceful curving lines perfect for both wreaths and bouquets

Uluhe forms dense thickets in the moist areas of Hawaii's volcanos. Pick when some fronds are fully opened and others are still curled into reddish brown heads. Air-dry both, or press the leaves lightly between sheets of paper. They will be more graceful if allowed to curve freely during drying.

WILLIAM S. MOYE

KENNETH SPENGLER

Genus/species: *Dictamnus albus*
Common name: gas plant
Perennial
Region: garden zones 3 through 8
Color: white, pink, and purple
  flowers; brown pods
Height: 2 feet (60 centimeters)
Arrangement: attractive
  background for tall or fan-shaped
  arrangements; pods good as
  accents on cone wreaths

Popular with gardeners for its compact growth and spires of flowers, gas plant provides elegant star-shaped pods for the arranger. They grow at the ends of short branchlets, close to a central stem, which makes them one of the more useful pod varieties in arrangements. If you pick the pods before the seeds are gone, you may be surprised to find the spring-like mechanism literally shooting the seeds across the room as the pods open!

Genus/species: *Digitalis purpurea*
Common name: foxglove
Annual, biennial, and perennial
Region: native to Europe, North
  Africa, and Near East; grown in
  temperate garden zones
Color: white, mauve, pink, purple,
  yellow, and apricot
Height: 2 to 5 feet (60 to 150
  centimeters)
Arrangement: Victorian-style
  arrangements

Foxglove quickly became a garden favorite and escaped to the wild in the American Northwest. It is now also bred in annual strains. Although the entire stalk can be dried, it is best to cut individual blossoms as they open and dry them face up in sand. They may then be glued back onto the stems. Since they tend to wilt in very humid weather, they may be sprayed lightly with fixative spray to make them more durable. If the blossoms are not cut, but left to fall naturally, a spire of very fine seedheads will form.

WILLIAM S. MOYE

Genus/species: *Dipsacus fullonum,*
D. sylvestris
Common name: teasel
Biennial
Region: native to Europe and North
America; grown in garden zones 3
through 9
Color: silver to lavender when
fresh; brown when dried
Height: 5 to 8 feet (1.5 to 2.4 meters)
Arrangement: an elegant addition
to wild or formal arrangements

In the Indian markets of the Andes,
bundles of teasel are still sold for
"teasing" or brushing wool fabric to
raise its nap. This use earned teasel a
place in early herb gardens, where it
is grown now for its attractive spiny
heads. In England, a favorite folk
craft is to make the heads into little
hedgehog decorations. Pick the
heads while they are in flower to preserve the silvery color, or allow them
to dry on the plant for pale tan
shades.

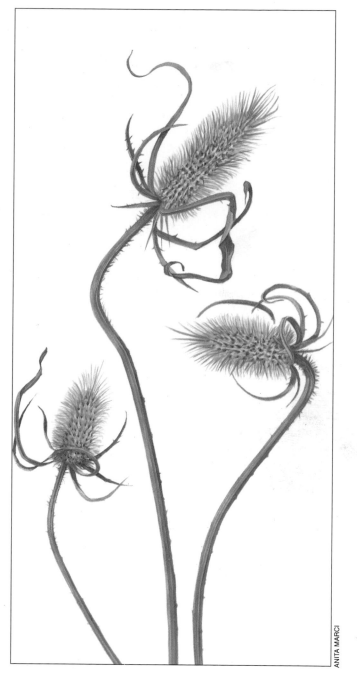

ANITA MARCI

WILLIAM S. MOYE

Genus/species: *Dodonaea eriocarpa, D. sandwickensis, D. viscosa*
Common name: hopseed, aalii
Shrub and tree
Region: native to Hawaii; might be grown successfully in Southern California and Florida
Color: pink-red
Height: up to 25 feet (7.6 meters)
Arrangement: beautiful seed clusters, ranging from mauve to rose, perfect as herbal wreath accents as well as in Victorian and other formal arrangements

There are a number of varieties of aalii growing all over Hawaii. They are characterized by small oval leaves, inconspicuous pink flowers, and seed capsules that grow in flower-like clusters. These have the rosy shades so hard to preserve in flowers, and so are invaluable in Edwardian and English-country bouquets as well as wreaths. Pick them at their colorful fruit stage and air-dry, hanging or standing.

Genus/species: *Echinocystis lobata*
Common name: wild cucumber,
mock cucumber
Annual
Region: native to North America;
grown in temperate garden zones
Color: white flowers, light brown
seed pods
Height: climbs to 20 feet (6 meters)
with support
Arrangement: seedpods and
tendrils add interest to modern
arrangements

Look for this wild vine in damp
thickets along the banks of streams.
Harvest the pods and tendril-covered
vines in early autumn. The stems are
very weak, so they are best used with
stronger material for support.

ANITA MARCI

ANITA MARCI

Genus/species: *Echinops exaltatus,*
  E. ritro
Common name: globe thistle, small
  globe thistle
Perennial
Region: garden zones 3 through 10
Color: purple
Height: 4 to 6 feet (1.2 to 1.8 meters)
Arrangement: combines well with
  soft pinks and gray foliage

Although its common name is globe
thistle, the *Echinops* is not even related to the thistles. The name comes
from its prickly qualities, which
make wearing gloves advisable while
picking it. Harvest it when the color
is a deep gray-blue but the tiny florets have not yet opened. Air-dry the
stalks by hanging, and treat them
carefully, since they are fairly fragile.
Leave on a few of the upper leaves,
which dry to a pale gray.

Genus/species: *Epilobium augustifolium*
Common name: fireweed
Perennial
Region: native to North America from Alaska to North Carolina
Color: pink to magenta
Height: up to 8 feet (2.4 meters)
Arrangement: good filler in any large arrangement

Fireweed is so named because it is frequently found in burned areas. After its blossoms fade, they form a spire of velvety seedpods up to two feet (sixty centimeters) tall. Pick these before they open and become a twisted mass of curled pods and seeds.

ANITA MARCI

Genus/species: *Eriophorum alpinum*

Common name: cotton grass, bog cotton

Perennial

Region: cool bogs of northern U.S. and Canada

Color: white

Height: 6 to 12 inches (15 to 30 centimeters)

Arrangement: showy clusters good against dark foliage

Cotton-like tufts of silky white bristles grow in numerous clusters, each at the end of a stalk. These may be dried by hanging upside down or standing in a dry vase. There are a number of varieties of this member of the sedge family that have similar silky tufts and are suitable for dried arrangements.

Genus/species: *Eryngium maritimum, E. alpinum*
Common name: sea holly
Perennial
Region: native to Europe and North America; garden zones 4 through 10
Color: blue-gray
Height: 2 to 6 feet (60 to 180 centimeters)
Arrangement: attractive with pinks, whites, and pale greens

The blue heads and stems of sea holly look as though they have been spray-painted, since the stems are an almost electric blue. Pick the blooms when they are fully open and hang them to dry. Since it grows on branching stems, it is best to pick individual blossoms at the point where the stem branches and wire them to longer stems if needed.

ANITA MARCI

ANITA MARCI

Genus/species: *Eucalyptus globulus, E. polyanthemos,* var.
Common name: gum tree, eucalyptus
Tree
Region: native to Australia; grown in California
Color: silvery, gray-green foliage
Height: 35 to 150 feet (10 to 45 meters)
Arrangement: provides good background foliage with broad coverage

Eucalyptus is one of the favorite preserved greens of florists. While there is wide variation in the size and shape of leaves, all are attractive and have a flowery fragrance that blends well with other scents. To preserve them, treat branches in glycerin, where they will maintain something of their original color and become leathery and flexible for arrangements. Along with the foliage, eucalyptus produces interesting pods for arrangements and cone wreaths.

ANITA MARCI

Genus/species: *Eupatorium maculatum, E. perfoliatum,* var.
Common name: boneset, Joe-Pye weed
Perennial
Region: native to the eastern U.S.; grown in garden zones 3 through 10
Color: blue, pink, purple, and white
Height: 2 to 6 feet (60 to 180 centimeters)
Arrangement: used mostly for large arrangements

Members of this genus are common wildflowers throughout much of eastern North America. All varieties should be picked before the fluffy flowers have begun to open, or they will shatter as they dry. Hang them loosely bundled to air-dry or dry individual heads face up in sand or silica gel.

Genus/species: *Euonymus*
   atropurpurea
Common name: euonymus,
   burning bush, wahoo
Hardy shrub
Region: native to eastern U.S.;
   grown in garden zones 3 through 9
Color: red leaves in fall
Height: 4 to 6 feet (1.2 to 1.8 meters)
Arrangement: sprays of small, red
   leaves good with holiday greens or
   as accents in richly colored
   arrangements

Euonymus is often planted along
the sides of highways. The leaves
vary from an almost translucent pink
to a rich maroon color, and they can
be dried by pressing entire sprays or
by treating them with glycerin. Look
also for the red seedpods. And keep
in mind that all parts of the shrub are
poisonous.

WILLIAM S. MOYE

WILLIAM S. MOYE

Genus/species: *Fagus grandiflora*
Common name: American beech
Forest tree
Region: eastern North America, as
   far west as Ontario and Texas
Color: green or yellow leaves;
   brown nuts
Height: 70 to 80 feet (21 to 24
   meters)
Arrangement: a favorite in
   Williamsburg-style or large,
   modern arrangements

Beech trees are easily recognized
by their bright green leaves with
straight parallel veins and by their
smooth, gray bark. Preserve in large
sprays by pressing between several
layers of paper, spreading leaves so
they do not overlap. Glycerin preservation first turns the leaves a deep
green, then a rich brown. Remove
from glycerin when they are the desired shade, then air-dry for a few
days. In the fall, gather beechnuts directly from the tree, where they
grow on short twigs close to main
stems. Beechnuts are small, attractive burrs, which are excellent in
cone wreaths and arrangements.

ANITA MARCI

Genus/species: *Filipendula hexapetala* (syn. *F. vulgaris*)
Common name: meadowsweet
Perennial
Region: garden zones 4 through 8
Color: white and pink
Height: 15 to 18 inches (38 to 45 centimeters)
Arrangement: combines well with pink roses, pink larkspur, and hydrangea (see pages 151, 63, and 103) for an English-country-style bouquet

Queen Elizabeth I favored meadowsweet as a strewing herb for its sweet smell, which assures it a place in the herb garden. It is an attractive border plant, and it also grows as a wildflower in many parts of the U.S. Air-dry the stems by standing or hanging. The smaller side shoots are good for miniature arrangements.

Genus/species: *Fougnieria splendens*
Common name: ocotillo, coach-whip, vine cactus, Jacob's staff
Cactus
Region: American Southwest
Color: brilliant red
Height: 6 to 10 feet (1.8 to 3 meters)
Arrangement: a good accent in medium and large bouquets

One of the few cacti that can be dried satisfactorily, ocotillo requires no more attention than simple hanging. The blossoms change shape slightly in air-drying, but the long spikes remain bright and dramatic in all types of arrangements. They are sometimes branched near the tip, which results in a fuller effect than the usual spikes.

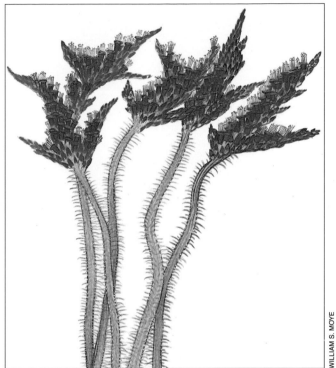

WILLIAM S. MOYE

MARY CLOSE

Genus/species: *Freesia refracta*
Common name: freesia
Perennial
Region: native to South Africa; grown in all temperate garden zones
Color: cream, yellow, pink, and mauve
Height: 18 inches (45 centimeters)
Arrangement: useful in many arrangement styles

These fragrant blossoms grow at right angles to the stem, and they should be dried separately, face up, in sand or silica gel. Wire or insert the blossom in a hollow stem to achieve the right height for any arrangement. The bulbs are hardy in garden zones nine and ten, and they may be forced to bloom indoors or grown as a houseplant anywhere.

Genus/species: *Fritillaria atropurpurea, F. pudica*
Common name: yellow fritillary, leopard lily, checkered lily
Perennial
Region: native to U.S. West; grown in garden zones 4 through 9
Color: dark purple and yellow
Height: 8 to 30 inches (20 to 76 centimeters)
Arrangement: purple flowers provide a good dark accent to arrangements of lighter flowers; both yellow and purple combine well with ferns for a woodland bouquet

A common wildflower in the Rockies, *Fritillaria* is also popular in gardens. Both the purple (*atropurpurea*) and yellow (*pudica*) varieties dry well. Insert a pin into the base of each flower before drying face up in sand. Reattach the blossoms to dried stems with the pin before arranging.

Genus/species: *Gaillardia aristata*
Common name: blanket flower, gaillardia
Annual and perennial
Region: native to western U.S., grown in temperate garden zones
Color: yellow and orange
Height: 1 to 2 feet (30 to 60 centimeters)
Arrangement: best in informal styles

This popular, daisy-like garden flower is descended from wild plants of western Canada and the U.S. and grows well in gardens throughout zones three through ten, blooming from early summer until frost. It is grown as an annual in northern zones. They dry well in sand, face up, and hold their color and shape well.

Genus/species: *Galax aphylla*
Common name: galax
Perennial
Region: native to the U.S. South;
grown in garden zones 3 through 9
Color: white flowers; deep green
foliage
Height: 6 to 12 inches (15 to 30
centimeters)
Arrangement: used as a covering
material to mask base supports
and florist's foam in arrangements

Usually found very deep in the forest, galax is also used as a ground cover in shaded areas. The leaves may be pressed or preserved in glycerin. The stems will often need to be wired in clusters to florist's picks to strengthen them. They are excellent camouflage material to cover lower stems and bases of arrangements.

ROMAN SZOLKOWSKI

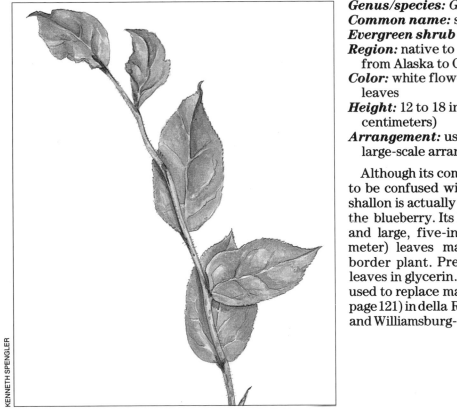

KENNETH SPENGLER

Genus/species: *Gaultheria shallon*
Common name: shallon, lemonleaf
Evergreen shrub
Region: native to North America
from Alaska to California
Color: white flowers; dark green
leaves
Height: 12 to 18 inches (30 to 45
centimeters)
Arrangement: used in dramatic,
large-scale arrangements

Although its common name leads it to be confused with the lemon tree, shallon is actually a heath, related to the blueberry. Its low growing habits and large, five-inch (thirteen-centimeter) leaves make it a favorite border plant. Preserve sprays of the leaves in glycerin. They may also be used to replace magnolia leaves (see page 121) in della Robbia style wreath and Williamsburg-style arrangements.

KENNETH SPENGLER

Genus/species: *Geranium grandiflorum, G. endressii*
Common name: cranesbill geranium
Perennial
Region: garden zones 4 through 9
Color: pink to light purple blossoms; tan pods
Height: 12 to 18 inches (30 to 45 centimeters)
Arrangement: seedpods attractive in delicate bouquets

This attractive, old-fashioned garden plant blooms throughout the summer. Let the blossoms drop from the plant, at which time long pointed seedheads form. When these open they curl back into small wood "flowers" that add a delicate note to arrangements. Press some of the leaves, too, for their deep-cut shape.

Genus/species: *Gladiolus* var.
Common name: gladiolus, sword
   lily
Perennial
Region: native to southern Europe
   and Africa; grown in temperate
   garden zones
Color: cream, yellow, orange, and
   red
Height: 3 to 4 feet (90 to 120
   centimeters)
Arrangement: flowers attractive in
   large arrangements, leaves in any
   type of arrangement

Dry blossoms individually, in sand.
Insert a pin in the base of each flower
and dust it with powdered chalk in a
matching color before drying. These
are not very sturdy and should be
handled carefully after drying. The
leaves, which are long and sword-
shaped, give rise to the name, based
on the Latin *gladius*, for sword.
Leaves may be dried by watering and
may remain green or turn shades of
brown and tan. They often assume
interesting shapes as they dry. Their
length makes them suitable for very
large works, but they may be cut to
any scale.

ROMAN SZOLKOWSKI

Genus/species: *Gleditsia triancanthos*
Common name: honey locust
Tree
Region: Mississippi Valley and the U.S. Midwest
Color: brown pods
Height: up to 140 feet (42 meters)
Arrangement: pods prized for their interesting, sculptured shapes that make them useful in modern arrangements or as accents in larger traditional arrangements

Not to be confused with the locusts that are members of the pea family, honey locust is actually a relative of the *Cassiae*. The pods are quite strong, and may be six or seven inches (fifteen to eighteen centimeters) long, so they can often be used by pushing them directly into the base material. This is such an attractive tree that it has become a favorite ornamental well outside its natural range.

Genus/species: *Godetia amoena, G. grandiflora*
Common name: satin flower, godetia
Annual
Region: native to western U.S.
Color: pink, white, red, and lavender
Height: 1 to 2 feet (30 to 60 centimeters)
Arrangement: whole stalk creates a showy effect

Godetia has cup-shaped blossoms that retain their satin sheen when dried in sand or silica gel. Place a pin in the base of each individual blossom, drying each as it blooms. Air-dry the stalk and pin or glue the dried blossoms back on. The blossoms may be grouped together or used singly on other stems.

MARY CLOSE

Genus/species: *Grevillea robusta*
Common name: silk oak, grevillea
Tree
Region: native to Australia; grown
in Southern California
Color: red, yellow, blue, and orange
Height: to 150 feet (45 meters)
Arrangement: used in free-form
arrangements or for color accent

Often grown as a houseplant, grevillea offers the look of a fern, but growing habits more adaptable to the home. As a tree, it grows well in all soil types. Dry the sprays in a vase with a little water, where they will take on the interesting curls and curves that make them so attractive in modern arrangements.

ANITA MARCI

Genus/species: *Gypsophila*
  paniculata, G. elegans
Common name: baby's breath
Annual and perennial
Region: native to Eurasia; grown in
  garden zones 3 through 10
Color: white and pink
Height: 18 to 36 inches (45 to 90
  centimeters)
Arrangement: used as a filler,
  especially with roses (see page
  151), for its delicate, airy texture

Although there is a tendency for florists to overuse baby's breath, it is still one of the most useful fillers for both fresh and dried arrangements. Its frothy quality makes it particularly useful with roses (see page 151), and *Dianthus*, as well as other small flowers in delicate colors. It is a stunning base for an all-white arrangement of *Lunaria*, hydrangea, and pearly everlasting (see pages 118, 103, and 26). It can be air-dried by hanging or preserved in glycerin. The latter solves its major problem for arrangers—its tendency to be very brittle and fragile when dried.

Genus/species: *Hakea cucullata*,
  var.
Common name: hakea
Evergreen shrub
Region: native to Australia; grown
  in Southern California
Color: green
Height: to 20 feet (6 meters)
Arrangement: used in
  arrangements with strong, bold
  designs

There are many species of hakea, of which those with cup-like leaves are the most useful to arrangers. It can be air-dried standing or hanging and is usually available from florist shops. Its somewhat strange shape and style make it better suited to large-scale, modern arrangements.

ROMAN SZOLKOWSKI

Genus/species: *Helichrysum bracteatum*
Common name: strawflower
Annual
Region: native to Australia; grown in garden zones 3 through 10
Color: yellow, orange, pink, red, and white
Height: 1 to 4 feet (30 to 120 centimeters)
Arrangement: used in all styles of arrangements for intense color and attractive shape

When most people think of dried flowers, it is the strawflower they picture. It is widely grown and sold by nearly every florist. Its wide range of colors and sizes makes it universally useful. Pick them before the flowers are fully open or the center will turn dark. Since its own stems do not dry well, the flower heads are picked as they bloom and are mounted on wires. Simply push the end of the wire up through the base of the stem and stand it in a basket to dry. As the flower loses moisture it closes on the wire, eventually holding it tightly. These wires are flexible and make placement of each bloom easy in arranging. Save the tiny blossoms for nosegays.

MARY CLOSE

ANITA MARCI

Genus/species: *Helipterum roseum, H. manglesii*

Common name: Swan River everlasting, sunray

Annual

Region: native to Australia and South Africa; garden zones 3 through 10

Color: pink and white petals; yellow centers

Height: 1 to 2 feet (30 to 60 centimeters)

Arrangement: used in small arrangements, especially with other pastels

The confusion over the proper classification of *Helipterum* is further compounded by the persistent use of the old classification names by seed houses. *H. manglesii* is also known as *rhodanthe*, and *H. roseum* is often listed as *Acrolinium roseum*, or simply as *Acrolinium*. Whatever their names, they are easy to grow and a fine addition to a dried flower bouquet. The stems of some of them tend to be weak, so they are often wired to stronger ones after drying. Although the flowers are already papery when blooming, they are best air-dried by hanging them in loose bundles.

Genus/species: *Helleborus foetidus,*
   H. angustifolius, H. orientalis
Common name: hellebore,
   Christmas rose, Lenten rose
Perennial
Region: garden zones 3 through 8
Color: white, green, and rose
Height: 18 to 24 inches (45 to 60
   centimeters)
Arrangement: leaves and flowers
   attractive with ferns for delicate
   spring arrangements

The hellebores are good for shaded
gardens, where they combine well
with ferns and hostas (see page 102).
Follow this theme through in arranging, combining the same plants. Press
leaves and dry the flowers in silica
gel. Be aware that all parts of the
plant are poisonous.

WILLIAM S. MOYE

KENNETH SPENGLER

Genus/species: *Heuchera sanguinea*
Common name: coralbells
Perennial
Region: garden zones 4 through 10
Color: pink, white, and red
Height: 12 to 18 inches (30 to 45 centimeters)
Arrangement: good in dainty, miniature arrangements or spiked in clusters

A native of the rocky ledges of the southwestern U.S. mountains, coralbells have become a garden favorite. Tiny pink bells grow from an arched stem, rising from a cluster of heart-shaped, bronze-colored leaves. Dry the flower stalks in sand and press the leaves. The flowers press well, too.

Genus/species: *Hordeum jubatum*
Common name: squirreltail barley,
squirreltail grass, foxtail grass
Annual and perennial
Region: native to Europe and Asia;
grown in temperate garden zones
Color: dries to wheat color
Height: 9 inches to 3 feet (23 to 90
centimeters)
Arrangement: fluffy seedheads
graceful in formal arrangements as
well as field bouquets

This variety of wild barley is common throughout the American West
as a weed. Cut it when the seedheads
are fluffy, and air-dry it hanging upside down. It is a perennial native of
North America whose beard is an upright fan of long, silky awns. All varieties are appropriate for nearly any
style of arrangement. This is a good
filler, and its soft tones look good
with pink and rose shades.

KENNETH SPENGLER

KENNETH SPENGLER

Genus/species: *Hosta caerulea, H. plantaginea,* var.

Common name: hosta, plantain lily

Perennial

Region: garden zones 3 through 9

Color: white, blue, and lavender

Height: 1 to 2 feet (30 to 60 centimeters)

Arrangement: wide leaves create an attractive frame in formal arrangements; seed stalks make elegant accents

Hosta is usually grown for its wide, richly colored leaves, which remain in tidy clumps all season. But its flowers can be quite attractive and, if left on the plant, form striking brown seedheads. The leaves are easily preserved by pressing lightly.

Genus/species: *Humulus lupulus*

Common name: hops

Perennial vine

Region: native to Eurasia; naturalized in North America south of garden zone 3

Color: pale green to brown

Height: to 25 feet (7.6 meters) with support

Arrangement: used for its graceful, sweeping curves in large arrangements and for the small, papery cones

Hops are difficult to harvest because of the prickly nature of the vines and leaves. Clusters of cones can often be removed fairly easily, however. It is best to arrange these vines, first removing the leaves, as soon after cutting as possible. Cones may be wired in clusters for use in more traditional arrangements.

ANITA MARCI

Genus/species: *Hydrangea paniculata grandiflora, H. macrophylla*
Common name: hydrangea
Perennial shrub
Region: Asian native; varieties grown in garden zones 3 through 10
Color: cream, pink, and blue
Height: up to 30 feet (9 meters)
Arrangement: a favorite in Victorian and Edwardian arrangements

Hydrangea is probably the most common ornamental shrub in North America, just as it has been popular in Europe for centuries and in Asia for centuries before that. The color of hydrangea depends upon the soil; blues result from acidic soil. Pick the flowers when they are fully bloomed and have begun to feel papery. Air-dry them standing in dry vases or hanging. Heads of this flower were a popular parlor bouquet in Victorian times, and they are still perfect for large, flamboyant arrangements. But individual clusters can be separated and wired to stems for use on a smaller scale. Wired to florist's picks, these are also perfect for herb wreaths. Combine hydrangea with *Lunaria* and white strawflowers (see pages 118 and 95) for a silvery white arrangement of great elegance.

ANITA MARCI

WILLIAM S. MOYE

Genus/species: *Hypericum perforatum*
Common name: Saint-John's-wort
Annual
Region: native to Europe; now grows wild throughout North America
Color: yellow blossoms; brown seeds
Height: 1 to 5 feet (30 to 150 centimeters)
Arrangement: large seed clusters good in wild bouquets or as an accent in more formal ones

This plant was brought to America by European immigrants who hung it in their windows on Saint John's Eve to keep bad spirits away. It grows as a weed with undistinguished yellow flowers that turn in the fall to rich, brown cupped seedpods on side branches off a central stem. These clusters may be five to six inches (thirteen to fifteen centimeters) wide, making them a dramatic addition to more formal arrangements.

Genus/species: *Iris sibirica, I. japonica,* var.
Common name: Siberian iris, iris
Perennial
Region: varieties suitable for garden zones 3 through 10, except the Gulf Coast
Color: white, yellow, purple, and mauve; brown when dried
Height: up to 4 feet (1.2 meters)
Arrangement: seedpods are elegant additions to formal and informal arrangements, as well as cone wreaths

While the blooms of all iris varieties are fragile and impossible to preserve, most produce striking seedheads if the flowers are not cut. The best of these are on the Siberian iris, but most others provide either round pods or long, slender capsules at the ends of the stems. Use them for elegant accents, as well as for filler on cone wreaths, where the long ones will fit well between larger cones to help cover the base.

ANITA MARCI

Genus/species: *Isatis tinctoria*
Common name: woad, dyer's woad
Biennial
Region: native to Europe; grown in garden zones 3 through 10
Color: yellow flowers; black seeds
Height: 3 to 4 feet (90 to 120 centimeters)
Arrangement: black seeds provide contrast and accent in brightly colored groupings

Woad earned its place in the herb garden as a dye plant; the leaves give a blue color to wool. The flowers are followed by black seeds that hang from the stem. Long a favorite of fresh arrangers, the seeds are often overlooked because they fall from the stem after a time. But if the flowers are placed upright in a dry container, the stalks will hold the seeds when they dry. If any should fall, a touch of glue will replace them.

WILLIAM S. MOYE

Genus/species: *Ixodia achilleodes*
Common name: Australian daisy
Perennial
Region: native to Australia
Color: white and cream
Height: 12 inches (30 centimeters)
Arrangement: most often used in
  miniature arrangements

The Australian daisy is usually available pre-dried from florists. It is a spring-blooming flower that air-dries easily. To use it in larger arrangements, simply wire several heads together onto a longer stem. It is also very attractive on herb wreaths.

Genus/species: *Kalmia latifolia*
Common name: mountain laurel, calico bush
Perennial shrub
Region: grows mostly in mountainous areas from the southeastern U.S. north into Canada
Color: pink blossoms; rich green leaves
Height: 4 to 8 feet (1.2 to 2.4 meters) north; 10 to 30 feet (3 to 9 meters) south
Arrangement: leaves prized for use in Williamsburg-style arrange-ments, also in swags and della-Robbia-style wreaths

Pick these elongated, shiny leaves in sprays and treat them in glycerin. They first become coppery, then turn dark brown, and should be removed when they have reached the desired color. Allow leaves to air-dry for several days before storing. Use natural stems for light arrangements or wire clusters to a single stem to achieve a fuller effect.

WILLIAM S. MOYE

WILLIAM S. MOYE

Genus/species: *Lagurus ovatus*
Common name: rabbit-tail grass, hare's-tail grass
Annual
Region: native to the Mediterranean; now grows wild on U.S. West Coast
Color: shades of buff
Height: 1 to 2 feet (30 to 60 centimeters)
Arrangement: wooly tufts blend nicely with harder seed pods to soften wild arrangements

The tufts of rabbit-tail grass may be as large as two inches (five centimeters) long, making them useful in larger displays, as well as smaller ones. Several may be wired in clusters for a showier effect. They take very well to dyeing, and they are especially attractive dyed in pastel shades. Be sure they are thoroughly dried on the plant when cut, and hang them to air-dry.

Genus/species: *Lathyrus maritimus*
Common name: beach pea
Perennial
Region: grows wild on northern seashores of North America, from New Jersey and Oregon to the Arctic, also along the Great Lakes
Color: purple blossoms; light brown pods
Height: 1 to 2 feet (30 to 60 centimeters)
Arrangement: clusters of tiny pods good for small arrangements

Beach peas are found growing in sand and resemble tiny garden peas, to which they are related. The pods should be allowed to dry at least partially on the vine. Clusters or individual pods are useful in cone wreaths and small arrangements.

KENNETH SPENGLER

Genus/species: *Laurus nobilis*
Common name: bay, sweet bay
Perennial
Region: native to Mediterranean;
   grown in temperate garden zones
Color: insignificant yellow blossoms;
   green leaves
Height: garden shrub 3 to 10 feet
   (0.9 to 3 meters), native 60 feet (18
   meters)
Arrangement: kitchen and herb
   wreaths, holiday arrangements

An aromatic evergreen, bay is perennial in outdoor gardens only in milder zones. Elsewhere it is planted in tubs that are brought inside for the winter. Partially dry the branches by hanging, then press them to flatten the leaves. Bay is an excellent material for wreaths if it is shaped while the branches are still supple, then allowed to dry in circular form. It also works well for swags.

ANITA MARCI

Genus/species: *Lavandula officinalis* (syn. *spica, vera*)
Common name: lavender
Perennial
Region: hardy in garden zones 5 through 10
Color: lavender
Height: up to 4 feet (1.2 meters) in warm climates
Arrangement: fine stems and tiny flowers best for miniatures and dainty nosegays

Known more for its distinctive scent than its ornamental uses, lavender is a mainstay of herb gardens. The fragrance lasts almost indefinitely. For ornamental use, pick lavender just as the spikes come into bloom, and hang it in small, loose bundles. Combine it with tiny white or light pink strawflowers (see page 97) and glycerin-treated acacia leaves for lovely nosegays.

Genus/species: *Lecythis usitata*
Common name: paradise nut,
  monkey pot tree, sapucaia
Tree
Region: northeastern South
  America and adjacent West Indies
Color: brown fruit
Height: 40 feet (12 meters)
Arrangement: clusters of pods add
  interest to modern arrangements
  and to seed and cone wreaths

The brown, woody capsules are known as monkey pots and have a small circular hole, which allows the wind to shake out the seeds as they ripen. Locals claim to catch monkeys by putting a few coarse sugar crystals into the holes. The monkey reaches for them, but his full hand will not fit through the hole so, rather than let go of the prize, he stays. Nuts grow in clusters, which should be gathered in the fall when they are brown and dry.

KENNETH SPENGLER

Genus/species: *Leontopodium
  alpinum*
Common name: edelweiss
Perennial
Region: native to the Alps; grown in
  garden zones 4 through 7
Color: white
Height: 6 inches (15 centimeters)
Arrangement: used in miniature
  arrangements

The fragile-looking edelweiss is actually quite sturdy. Pick it before the fluffy centers have begun to open, and dry it face up on a wire mesh with the stems hanging through. It is not difficult to grow, but it requires good drainage for its roots.

ANITA MARCI

MARY CLOSE

Genus/species: *Liatris punctata, L. spicata*

Common name: blazing star, gayfeather

Perennial

Region: native to North America from Manitoba to Texas; grown in garden zones 3 through 10

Color: pink, orchid, and purple

Height: 2 to 6 feet (30 to 180 centimeters)

Arrangement: used in large arrangements for its dramatic spikes of color

Liatris, unlike most spikes of flowers, blooms from the top downward. Pick stalks before the topmost flowers begin to fade and dry them by hanging. They hold their bright color and firm shape for years when dried. *Liatris* is a good choice for gardeners in arid zones, since its taproot may be as long as fifteen feet (four and one-half meters), and it is able to search for water at a far greater depth than most plants. This does, of course, make *Liatris* almost impossible to transplant once it is an established plant.

Genus/species: *Limonium latifolium*

Common name: German statice, perennial statice (also called sea lavender)

Perennial

Region: native to Europe; garden zones 3 through 10

Color: white to mauve

Height: 18 to 24 inches (45 to 60 centimeters)

Arrangement: used as filler in arrangements and wreaths

Very similar in appearance to *L. carolinianum*, the flowers on *L. latifolium* are larger, more open, and lighter in color. The stems are heavier and more brittle while growing, but sturdier than the tidal varieties once they are dried. Plant it in a part of the garden where it can remain for many years. It will begin blooming the second year. To dry it, cut and hang the stalks with each of the wide heads hung separately to avoid crushing. The heads are so wide that they are normally broken into smaller clusters, which are wired to longer stems for arranging.

ANITA MARCI

MARY CLOSE

Genus/species: *Limonium sinuatum*

Common name: annual statice

Annual

Region: native to Mediterranean; grown in garden zones 3 through 10

Color: pink, white, purple, blue, and salmon

Height: 18 to 24 inches (45 to 60 centimeters)

Arrangement: used in nearly every style of arrangement for its bright colors and strong shapes

Next to the strawflowers, this statice is probably the most common dried flower. It is also used fresh in arrangements, so look for it in florist's bouquets and remove it to a dry vase as soon as the rest of the flowers have faded. In the garden, cut it when the flowers are fully bloomed and hang or stand the stalks to dry. The stems of statice are very strong, but the florets tend to fall if treated roughly. The may be reattached with a drop of glue.

Genus/species: *Linum perenne*
Common name: perennial flax
Perennial
Region: garden zones 4 through 10
Color: blue
Height: 1 to 3 feet (30 to 90
   centimeters)
Arrangement: lends an airy touch
   to arrangements

Although the dainty blue flowers
are far too fragile to preserve, if left
in the garden flax will develop a series of wonderful little tan balls along
the stems. These add an airy filler to
small arrangements.

WILLIAM S. MOYE

KENNETH SPENGLER

Genus/species: *Liquidambar styraciflua*
Common name: sweet gum
Tree
Region: southern New England south to the Gulf Coast
Color: red leaves in fall; brown seeds
Height: up to 150 feet (45 meters)
Arrangement: seedpods are perfect additions to all cone wreaths and decorations

Although sweet gum may be considered a nuisance by many who must rake its numerous bristly seedpods from lawns in the fall, it is a favorite tree for anyone who makes cone wreaths or other decorations. The brown pods look like wooden thistles, perfectly round, and up to two inches (five centimeters) in diameter. The leaves turn bright red in the fall and may be dried by pressing between sheets of paper. Their star shape is a favorite in Williamsburg-style arrangements.

Genus/species: *Livistona chinensis*
Common name: Chinese fan palm
Perennial
Region: native to China; grown as a house plant in North America
Color: green, dries to light green or cream
Height: up to 30 feet (9 meters)
Arrangement: useful as background or filler

Livistona is only one of many palms that are easily dried by pressing or hanging. Nearly all are useful to the arranger. Some have thin, almost wispy leaves, which are best dried standing or hanging to allow leaves to curl naturally. Nearly any palm with a reasonable-sized leaf is worth drying. The fan-shaped palms are especially good for background foliage.

KENNETH SPENGLER

Genus/species: *Lobularia maritima,* var.
Common name: sweet alyssum
Perennial
Region: garden zones 3 through 8
Color: pink and white
Height: 3 to 12 inches (7 to 30 centimeters)
Arrangement: clusters are best for miniature pieces; may be grouped and wired to longer stems for larger arrangements

Although these are perennials, they are grown as annuals in most gardens, where they will bloom throughout the whole summer. Pick the fragrant clusters of sweet alyssum just before they are fully bloomed, and dry them face up in sand or silica gel. They are fragile and must be handled carefully, but they hold up well in a bouquet.

WILLIAM S. MOYE

ANITA MARCI

Genus/species: *Lunaria annua*
Common name: money plant,
honesty, silver dollar
Biennial
Region: all temperate garden zones
Color: purple flowers; silver-white
pods
Height: 12 to 30 inches (30 to 75
centimeters)
Arrangement: beautiful with red
rose, (see page 151) cornflower,
and larkspur (see page 63), for a
delicate and airy effect, or with
carlina, moluccella, and white
strawflower (see pages 49
and 97) for an elegant, warm
cream-colored arrangement

To most of us, lunaria bespeaks Victorian. Its silver discs give an ethereal look to arrangements, and it was a great favorite in England's Victorian arrangements long before it became popular in the U.S. The best silver color is obtained by picking the stems when the pods start to turn brown, then removing the outer coverings by hand. This will occur naturally, but the inner silver circles may darken or be damaged in the process. *Lunaria* is also stunning when combined with dark red roses and deep green ferns, perhaps with pearly everlasting.

Genus/species: *Lycopodium cernuun, L. clavatum,* var.
Common name: club moss
Perennial
Region: varieties grown in garden zones 3 through 10
Color: green
Height: up to 1 foot (30 centimeters)
Arrangement: used as a background and filler, especially in holiday arrangements

Members of this genus of low-growing evergreens grow in most parts of the world, from the tropics to arctic zones. While the plants may grow to several feet (one meter) in length, they never grow far off the ground, hence their common name reference to moss. Dry it hanging or in a vase, or treat it with glycerin. It is often used as a background for red berries, holly, and cones in Christmas arrangements, but it makes an equally suitable background for delicate spring flowers such as lily-of-the-valley and *Dianthus* varieties (see pages 64 and 75).

ROMAN SZOLKOWSKI

WILLIAM S. MOYE

Genus/species: *Lythrum salicaria*
Common name: purple loosestrife
Perennial
Region: native to Europe; now grows wild in North America
Color: reddish purple
Height: 18 to 48 inches (45 to 120 centimeters); wild to 6 feet (1.8 meters)
Arrangement: dramatic spikes good for larger styles

Varieties of this hardy plant thrive throughout North America where there were a few native strains before the European plant was introduced. Pick the spikes before the top buds are open and hang them separately to air-dry. The color will evolve to a rich, dark purple, and the natural stem will remain firm and sturdy. They lend grace and style to fan-shaped formal arrangements and are just as useful in informal country bouquets.

Genus/species: *Magnolia grandiflora*
Common name: southern magnolia
Tree
Region: common to American Deep South
Color: white blossoms; deep green leaves
Height: 60 to 80 feet (18 to 24 meters)
Arrangement: leaves attractive in Williamsburg- or della Robbia-style arrangements

The magnolia has become the symbol of the American South where spreading boughs are graceful and beautiful all year round. The leaves turn brown, then black, in glycerin, and they become soft and pliable as well. For this reason, it is often necessary to wire their backs so they will stand up. Magnolia leaves provide the dark fan background we associate with the formal Williamsburg-style arrangements, but they are equally useful in modern pieces. The leaves may also be pressed. The magnolia tree has a very attractive cone-like fruit, which is highly prized for cone wreaths and arrangements. These can be wired in clusters for use in larger bouquets as well.

WILLIAM S. MOYE

KENNETH SPENGLER

Genus/species: *Malus pumila*
Common name: apple
Hardy tree
Region: native to Asia Minor; grows throughout North America except in high elevations and arid areas
Color: white blossoms with a pink tinge
Height: 20 to 40 feet (6 to 12 meters)
Arrangement: branches good in Oriental arrangements; flower clusters useful in all arrangement styles

Perhaps the most popular of all temperate climate fruits, the apple was cultivated over 2000 years ago, spread to Britain with the Roman legions, thence to America, where it moved west with the settlers. Its spring blossoms are easily dried face up in sand. Carefully remove clusters, including some foliage, and insert a pin through the back before drying. Clusters can then be reattached to the branch after drying. Or, they may be attached to straight stems for use in traditional arrangements.

Genus/species: *Marrubium*
vulgare
Common name: horehound
Perennial
Region: garden zones 3 through 10
Color: velvety-gray leaves and
seedheads
Height: 2 to 3 feet (60 to 90
centimeters)
Arrangement: used for wreath
bases

Horehound's place in the herb garden was secured long ago by its medicinal ability to soothe sore throats.
It is still made into candies for this
purpose. Although it can be used in
arrangements, its primary interest
here is as an easily twined base for
herb wreaths. Wind it onto a wire
frame while it is fresh and supple,
wiring it loosely to hold in place.
Horehound is usually combined with
a heavier material such as lamb's ears
or artemisia (see page 32) for wreaths.

ANITA MARCI

MARY CLOSE

Genus/species: *Matthiola incana annua*

Common name: stock

Annual, biennial, and perennial

Region: native to Mediterranean; grown in temperate garden zones

Color: cream, pink, mauve, purple, yellow, and crimson

Height: 1 to 3 feet (30 to 90 centimeters)

Arrangement: spikes good as a background or an accent, depending on the color and size of arrangement

Stock is among the most useful plants in fresh arranging, and is equally useful when dried. Its wide variety of colors and densely flowered spikes make a good accent or primary flower in most arrangement styles. Dry the entire stalk face down in sand.

Genus/species: *Melaleuca gibbosa,*
  M. incana
Common name: melaleuca,
  honeymyrtle, bottlebrush
Perennial
Region: native to Australia
Color: mauve, gray, silver, and
  yellow
Height: 3 to 6 feet (90 to 180
  centimeters)
Arrangement: adds interest to any
  arrangement because of its
  unusual shape

Melaleuca looks like a very fine,
round thistle growing at the end of a
stem covered with delicate leaves.
The *incana* variety has yellow
flowers and pale gray foliage. Dry the
seedheads by hanging them in loose
bundles. Despite its common name of
bottlebrush, it should not be confused with *Callistemon* (see page 42).

KENNETH SPENGLER

WILLIAM S. MOYE

Genus/species: *Mertensia virginica*
Common name: Virginia bluebell
Perennial
Region: native to Virginia; grows in woodlands of eastern U.S.
Color: blue blossoms; pink buds
Height: 1 to 2 feet (30 to 60 centimeters)
Arrangement: hanging clusters work well in all types of bouquets

Clusters of inch-long (two-centimeter) trumpets hang from stems, making a graceful accent in arrangements. Dry these in sand, leaving the flowers on the stem. Gently fill bells with sand to hold their shape.

Genus/species: *Metrosideros collinus*
Common name: ohia-lehua, liko-lehua
Tree
Region: native to Hawaii; can be grown in Southern California and Florida
Color: mostly red, also orange, yellow, and white
Height: to 80 feet (24 meters)
Arrangement: bright accent for any style of arrangement

This is the most common tree in the parks of Hawaii, growing from sea level to elevations of 8000 feet (2400 meters) on Mauna Loa. The leaves often have an underside coating of dense white hairs, giving them a velvety texture. The clusters of red flowers have long, protruding stamens, which dry surprisingly well considering their apparent fragility. They retain their bright color as well as their strength after air-drying. Pick and dry the buds also, and the tiny whitish clusters of new leaves at the stem tips, which are excellent for herb wreaths.

WILLIAM S. MOYE

Genus/species: *Moluccella laevis*
Common name: bells of Ireland
Annual
Region: Mediterranean native;
 grown in temperate garden zones
Color: green, dries to parchment
Height: 18 to 36 inches (45 to 90
 centimeters)
Arrangement: combines well with
 white strawflowers and fluffy
 grass heads

Not flowers at all, the bells of *Mo-luccella* are really enlarged calyxes. It requires a long growing season, so northern gardeners should plant indoors early in the spring. Only the mature calyxes dry well, so be sure the plant is mature before cutting. If the bells should fall from the stalk, attach them with a drop of glue at the base of each. Air-dry by hanging each stalk separately.

MARY CLOSE

ANITA MARCI

Genus/species: *Monarda didyma, M. fistulosa*

Common name: bee balm, wild bergamot

Perennial

Region: American native; grown in garden zones 4 through 9

Color: red, pink, lavender, and white

Height: 2 to 5 feet (60 to 150 centimeters)

Arrangement: button-like heads used in arrangements of all styles and on herb wreaths

Unfortunately, the brilliant colors of bee balm are lost in drying, but the brown compact heads are still very attractive. Bee balm is grown in herb gardens as a tea plant, and it is a favorite of both bees and hummingbirds.

Genus/species: *Muscari armeniacum*
Common name: grape hyacinth
Perennial
Region: garden zones 2 through 10
Color: blue; dries to pale grey
Height: 6 to 9 inches (15 to 23 centimeters)
Arrangement: seed stalks useful in miniature arrangements

The tiny spikes of silvery seedpods left after the blooms have fallen are easy to overlook in the garden. But they are so useful in small-scale arrangements that it would be a shame to waste them. Allow the seeds to form, then cut and finish air-drying by standing them loosely in a dry vase.

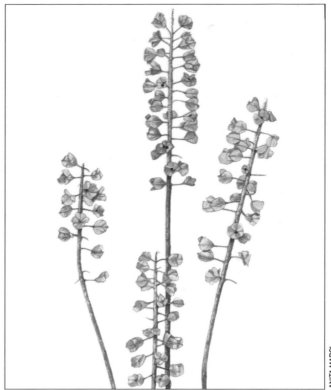

ANITA MARCI

WILLIAM S. MOYE

Genus/species: *Myosotis scorpioides semperflorens, M. oblongata*
Common name: forget-me-not
Annual, biennial, and perennial
Region: native to Europe and north Asia; now grows wild throughout much of U.S.
Color: blue, also pink and white
Height: up to 12 inches (30 centimeters)
Arrangement: good in miniature arrangements, or spiked in clusters for larger arrangements

Pick only a few of these delicate plants at a time and process them quickly since they wilt rapidly. Before drying, shake them in powdered blue chalk to stabilize the color. Dry face up in sand or silica gel, then replace the yellow center with a tiny drop of yellow oil or acrylic paint. Although these are perennial in their natural habitat, they are sometimes treated as annuals or biennials in the garden.

WILLIAM S. MOYE

Genus/species: *Myrica cerifera*
Common name: bay, bayberry wax myrtle, candleberry
Perennial
Region: native to temperate coastal areas of the U.S.
Color: pale blue berries
Height: 4 to 5 feet (1.2 to 1.5 meters), may grow to 30 feet (9 meters)
Arrangement: berry spikes attractive in modern or traditional settings

These shrubs are the source of wax for traditional candles, but their spikes make a nice addition to bouquets. Cut the stems at first frost, clipping off leaves. Hang dry the stalk with its close covering of berries for about two weeks. The leaves may also be dried, but they do not retain their green color for bouquets. Their fragrance is a pleasant addition to potpourri, however.

Genus/species: *Narcissus incomparabilis, N. jonquilla,* var.
Common name: narcissus, daffodil, jonquil
Perennial
Region: garden zones 4 through 10
Color: white, yellow, and orange
Height: 1 to 2 feet (30 to 60 centimeters)
Arrangement: provides a bright accent in spring bouquets; combines well with pussy willow sprays

The varieties of jonquil, narcissus, and daffodil have been so interbred that the old distinctions have little meaning any more. It is correct to refer to all three under the name of narcissus. Unlike most other heavy-textured bulb flowers, they dry quite well, especially in sand or silica gel. But even laid on a screen in a dry place they will hold their shape and color well enough to be used in arrangements. Clusters of the smaller types dried in dessicants are excellent accents for large herb wreaths.

MARY CLOSE

WILLIAM S. MOYE

Genus/species: *Nelumbo nucifera*
Common name: lotus, sacred lotus, East Indian lotus
Perennial
Region: native to Asia and the Nile Valley; winter hardy where underwater roots are below frost line
Color: pink flowers; brown fruit
Height: up to 1 foot (30 centimeters) above water surface
Arrangement: dried fruit useful as an accent in large and modern arrangements

The sacred lotus of India has enormous symbolic meaning in many Eastern religions, but it is of interest to the flower arranger for its large, flat-topped fruit. The fruit is a disc-shaped receptacle with hard nuts contained in pits on the upper surface. The entire pod floats face down in the water for weeks until the edges of the holes rot one by one and drop the seeds. The wind moves the fruit along the surface of a river, allowing one pod to travel great distances and drop its seeds over a large area. The pods may be purchased in floral supply shops.

Genus/species: *Nigella damascena*
Common name: love-in-a-mist
Annual
Region: Mediterranean native;
grown in temperate garden zones
Color: blue, lavender, pink, and
white; dries to pale brown
Height: 12 to 18 inches (30 to 45
centimeters)
Arrangement: combines nicely
with delicate flowers

Nigella's flowers are followed by
pale green, papery seedpods, each at
the end of a stem. These are often
tinged with reddish markings, which
make them even more attractive in
arrangements. Since they are not easily transplanted, it is best to sow seeds
very early in the spring or the pre-
vious fall. They will self-seed in sub-
sequent years if a few pods are left on
the plant in the fall. To dry, cut when
pods are mature and hang upside
down. Leave on the foliage near the
pods.

ANITA MARCI

WILLIAM S. MOYE

Genus/species: *Oenothera biennis*
Common name: evening primrose
Biennial
Region: native to temperate garden
zones and South America
Color: yellow flowers; brown pods
Height: 1 to 2 feet (30 to 60
centimeters)
Arrangement: pods useful in cone
wreaths or as an accent in all
arrangement styles

In summer these attractive yellow
blossoms open in the late afternoon
and evening, hence the common
name, evening primrose. If left unpicked, the stalks develop seed pods
of a long tulip shape with pointed,
outward-curving petals. They resemble little flowers carved from wood
and are striking in all kinds of arrangements.

ANITA MARCI

Genus/species: *Origanum vulgare, O. onites*
Common name: pot marjoram
Annual
Region: Mediterranean native; grown in garden zones 3 through 10
Color: pink to magenta
Height: 2 to 3 feet (30 to 60 centimeters)
Arrangement: provides good color in any arrangement, especially with artemisia (see page 32) or other gray foliage

The confusion over the varieties of oregano and marjoram nomenclature extends even to botanists. There are several differing opinions on how they should be classed, but the main thing to know is how to tell the culinary varieties from the purely decorative ones. If you are buying seeds, you must simply hope for the best, but if you are buying plants, insist on tasting a leaf. If it has a definite flavor, it is one of the culinary varieties. If it has a faint or no flavor, it is pot marjoram. The flowers grow in clusters at the ends of branched stems and darken as they dry to a rich pink or rosy purple. The stems are sturdy, and the flowers will keep for years if simply cut and stood in a dry vase. Culinary marjoram (*O. majorana*) has lighter flowers on shorter stems, but it also dries well.

Genus/species: *Ornithogalum thyrsoides*
Common name: chincherinchee
Perennial
Region: garden zones 7 through 10
Color: white
Height: 9 to 18 inches (23 to 45 centimeters)
Arrangement: Useful with other white or pastel flowers

This is one of the few flowers that responds better to drying after it has been kept in water. Allow the individual florets to open about two-thirds of the way up the stem, then dry in silica gel or sand.

KENNETH SPENGLER

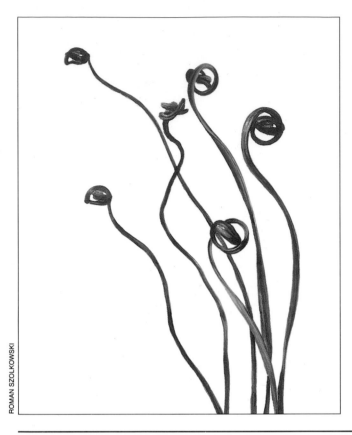

ROMAN SZOLKOWSKI

Genus/species: *Osmunda cinnamomea*
Common name: cinnamon fern
Perennial
Region: native to eastern U.S.
Color: green
Height: up to 3 feet (90 centimeters)
Arrangement: used as foliage with roses (see page 151) or with hosta and hellebore in woodland arrangements (see pages 102 and 99)

This is only one of the wide variety of ferns that grow in nearly every climate of the earth. They are highly useful to both fresh and dried flower arrangers. They may be treated in glycerin or pressed between layers of newspaper. Since most ferns prefer moist, shaded places, they are frequently grown by gardeners whose land has little sun. They are good background in fan-shaped arrangements and as foliage with any white flower. All dried ferns are fragile, except those that have been treated with glycerin.

Genus/species: *Oxytropis lambertii*
Common name: locoweed
Perennial
Region: native to arid regions of western U.S.
Color: rosy blossoms; gray-green foliage
Height: 6 to 18 inches (15 to 45 centimeters)
Arrangement: soft colors good in English-country-style arrangements

This legume contains a narcotic, which makes it dangerous to grazing animals. Remove flowers and insert pins, then dry face up in sand. Sift powdered white chalk over the rest of the plant and dry it in sand, lying on its side. When both are dry, replace blossoms on stem. If left in the field, locoweed develops short beans, which grow off the stems at intervals. These may also be dried for arrangements.

WILLIAM S. MOYE

Genus/species: *Paeonia lactiflora,*
P. suffruticosa

Common name: peony, Chinese
peony, common garden peony, tree
peony

Perennial

Region: Asian native; grown in
garden zones 3 through 8 and on
the U.S. West Coast portions of
zone 9

Color: pink, white, and red

Height: 2 to 4 feet (60 to 120
centimeters)

Arrangement: used in large,
dramatic arrangements

Peonies are among the most difficult flowers to dry, but the results are
so spectacular in arrangements that it
is well worth the effort. Choose single or semi-double varieties and dry
them face up in silica gel. Make sure
that it sifts down into the crevices between the petals, and that the entire
flower is covered. Leave only enough
stem so that is can be wired after drying.

MARY CLOSE

ANITA MARCI

Genus/species: Papaver somniferum, P. orientale, var.
Common name: poppy, opium poppy, Oriental poppy
Perennial
Region: native to Europe and Asia; grown in garden zones 2 through 9
Color: pink, red, and orange flowers; light brown pods
Height: 10 to 30 inches (25 to 75 centimeters)
Arrangement: seedheads useful in all arrangement styles, especially combined with oats or grasses for an elegant harvest wreath or bouquet

It seems only fair that the poppy, one of the garden's most short-lived flowers, should leave us some permanent memento of the care we lavish upon it . The seedpods would be worth raising poppies for, even without the bloom, for they are symmetrical and attractive as well as sturdy and long-lasting. Some varieties form a longer, bean-like pod, but most are fairly round. Allow the petals to fall, leaving the flower stalk until pod is well-formed and dry.

Genus/species: *Pennisetum ruppelii, P. villosum*

Common name: fountain grass, feathertop

Annual

Region: native to Ethiopia; grown in temperate garden zones

Color: rose, lavender, and red to brown

Height: 2 to 4 feet (30 to 120 centimeters)

Arrangement: lends a feathery quality to almost any style

Both varieties of this grass are easily grown in most climates, and will grow as tender perennials in the tropics. Cut the plumes when they are fully open and hang them upside down to dry. The Victorians were very fond of these plumes, which are still popular because they lend grace to a variety of displays, from wild to modern to formal.

KENNETH SPENGLER

KENNETH SPENGLER

Genus/species: *Penstemon hirsutus, P. gloxinioides*

Common name: hairy beard-tongue, beard-tongue

Perennial and annual

Region: garden zones 6 through 10

Color: blue, also pink, mauve, red, and green

Height: 1 to 3 feet (30 to 90 centimeters), depending on variety

Arrangement: flowers appropriate for almost any style; seedpods best for wild or more modern styles

In cooler zones these plants are best started indoors so they will have time to bloom and seed before frost. Blue varieties provide one of the best, most long-lasting blue tones when dried. The entire plant should be dried in sand, lying on its side. The seedpods, which grow in clusters on tall branching stems, may be air-dried by hanging. Although the entire stalk of flowers or seeds is fairly large, small side shoots of either may be broken off and wired to stems for use in smaller arrangements.

WILLIAM S. MOYE

Genus/species: *Petalostemon purpureum*
Common name: prairie clover
Perennial
Region: native to the American prairies
Color: purple
Height: up to 2 feet (60 centimeters)
Arrangement: rich color makes this perfect as an accent or for use in combination with other blues and purples

The blossoms of prairie clover resemble the coneflower and bloom wild in summer. The roots are very deep, making them difficult to transplant, but this makes them perfect for growing in arid climates. Air-dry the flowers by hanging singly.

Genus/species: *Phacelia campanularia*
Common name: California bluebell
Annual
Region: native to western U.S.; grown in garden zones 3 through 8
Color: blue
Height: 8 to 10 inches (20 to 25 centimeters)
Arrangement: perfect for accent and color in many arrangements

These small flowers can be wired in clusters to longer stems for use in larger arrangements, but their delicate bells are also perfect for miniature and airy arrangements. To prevent them from becoming transparent when dry, brush them lightly with powdered blue chalk before drying face up in sand.

WILLIAM S. MOYE

KENNETH SPENGLER

Genus/species: *Philadelphus coronarius*
Common name: mock orange, syringa
Deciduous shrub
Region: native to central and southern Europe; grown in mild temperate garden zones
Color: white
Height: 5 to 7 feet (1.5 to 2 meters)
Arrangement: one of best white blossoms for arrangements of all kinds

The scent of mock orange has made it a favorite ornamental to plant near porches and windows. It blooms profusely in summer, and the individual blossoms, or clusters of them, should be dried in sand, face up. They can be returned to the original branch with pins or glue, or wired to upright stems for use in more traditional arrangements. They stay a pure white, which makes them particularly good flowers to preserve.

Genus/species: *Phlomis fruticosa*
Common name: Jerusalem sage
Perennial
Region: garden zone 9
Color: silver and yellow
Height: 12 to 18 inches (30 to 45 centimeters)
Arrangement: long-stemmed clusters striking as accents or in autumn bouquets or wreaths

The candelabra-shaped heads of Jerusalem sage are particularly useful because of their long stems. The wrinkled, gray leaves act as a platform to frame and support the clusters of blossoms. Air-dry the flowers by hanging them or standing them in a dry vase. Press the leaves lightly or hang to dry. Seedheads form if the flowers are allowed to remain on the plant, and these too are attractive in arrangements.

KENNETH SPENGLER

Genus/species: *Phormium tenax*
Common name: New Zealand flax
Perennial
Region: native to New Zealand;
    grown in U.S. West Coast gardens
Color: red, bronze, and purple
    leaves
Height: 4 to 8 feet (1.2 to 2.4 meters)
Arrangement: fan-shaped sprays
    are good as background in very
    large pieces; seed spikes dramatic
    in modern arrangements

The sword-shaped leaves of New
Zealand flax fan out in a dramatic display in the garden and retain their
form when pressed lightly until dry.
They are too big for many arrangements, but they make a perfect background for large spaces. Individual
leaves may be cut to shorter lengths
for smaller arrangements. The full
red flowers mature into brown seedpods set on zigzag stalks that can be
air-dried.

KENNETH SPENGLER

Genus/species: *Physalis alkekengi*
Common name: Chinese lantern
Perennial
Region: native to Asia; grown in garden zones 3 through 10
Color: orange
Height: 1 to 2 feet (30 to 60 centimeters)
Arrangement: used as a bright accent in harvest bouquets

Chinese lantern should be planted where it will not overrun an entire garden, since it spreads quickly and deeply with runners in every direction. Cut stems when lanterns are brightly colored and a few are still green. Remove the leaves and hang the stalks right side up by hooking the top lanterns over a line. They should not be gathered into bundles or hung upside down, since the lanterns should hang naturally.

Genus/species: *Podocarpus macrophyllus*
Common name: southern yew
Tree or shrub
Region: native of Japan; grown in U.S. from North Carolina southward
Color: green
Height: up to 60 feet (18 meters)
Arrangement: used as foliage and filler

Podocarpus is not really a yew, although they are related. The flat needles are somewhat longer than those of yew, and it is not as well suited to northern climates. It may be air-dried or preserved in glycerin, where it may take on red or yellow striations that add to its usefulness in arrangements.

ROMAN SZOLKOWSKI

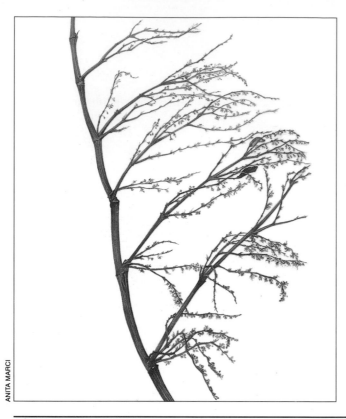

ANITA MARCI

Genus/species: *Polygonum cuspidatum, P. aubertii, P. capitatum*
Common name: Japanese knotweed, silver-lace vine
Perennial
Region: Asian native; naturalized in garden zones 3 through 10
Color: white flowers; dries to brown
Height: vines may grow 30 feet (9 meters) in a year
Arrangement: used as a frame for large arrangements, filler for smaller ones

P. cuspidatum was brought to North America as an ornamental, but it soon proved impossible to control. The other varieties are still planted to cover fences and banks, and are easily controlled. All bloom with white or pinkish panicles of flowers, which should be picked at their peak. Remove the leaves and air-dry the stems and flowers by hanging.

Genus/species: *Potentilla recta, P. norvegica*
Common name: cinquefoil, rough-fruited cinquefoil
Annual and biennial
Region: grows wild throughout eastern U.S. along roadsides and fields
Color: yellow blossoms; green buds; brown pods
Height: 1 to 2 feet (30 to 60 centimeters)
Arrangement: leaves and buds good as filler; seedpods nice as accents

The unopened buds and hairy-looking leaves of cinquefoil provide excellent greens when air-dried by hanging. They can be wired into clusters of two or three. When dried in the field, the cup-shaped flower heads turn brown. Each stem has an open branched top making an attractive spray of pods for arranging. Cinquefoil can be gathered in the field even in winter, for it is quite sturdy.

WILLIAM S. MOYE

Genus/species: *Proboscidea louisianica*
Common name: unicorn plant, devil's-claw
Annual
Region: native to the south-central U.S.; grown in garden zones 3 through 7
Color: white, lavender, and pink flowers; brown pods
Height: 2 to 3 feet (60 to 90 centimeters)
Arrangement: used for dramatic accent in modern arrangements

Unicorn plant is grown in gardens for its strange seedpod, which can be as long as six inches (fifteen centimeters). Dry the stems with pods attached by hanging them upside down. The pods split in half as the seeds ripen. Plant them indoors early in the season in northern zones, directly in the garden in southern areas.

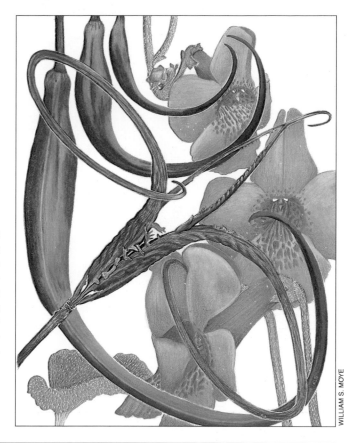

WILLIAM S. MOYE

ROMAN SZOLKOWSKI

Genus/species: *Protea compacta, P. neriifolia,* var.
Common name: protea
Shrub and small tree
Region: native to Africa and Australia; some grown in California
Color: browns and pinks
Height: to 60 feet (3 meters) or more
Arrangement: used in modern arrangements

There are many different varieties of protea available from the florist, and they rarely have species names, so it is simply a matter of shopping until you find those you like. Many of them are as large six to eight inches (15 to 20 centimeters) in diameter, but a few smaller ones are available. Since they are rather heavy and commanding in appearance, they are best used as accents in large contemporary arrangements. They air-dry easily hanging or lying on a screen.

WILLIAM S. MOYE

Genus/species: *Quercus coccinea*
Common name: scarlet oak
Tree
Region: grows from eastern central
    U.S. north to southern New
    England
Color: new leaves bright red,
    mature dark red
Height: up to 70 feet (21 meters)
Arrangement: tiny leaves perfect
    for miniatures and as foliage in
    larger pieces

The sharp-toothed leaves of the
scarlet oak are a beautiful red when
they first emerge, tiny and perfectly
shaped. Press sprays, spreading
leaves carefully so they do not overlap as they dry. Larger sprays of full-
grown leaves may be pressed, too.
Treating in glycerin changes the color
but renders the leaves more supple
and easier to arrange. Sprays of tiny
scarlet oak, treated in glycerin, are
often available from florists and floral suppliers. Acorns from these
trees, although hard to wire for arrangements, can be used on wreaths
where they can be glued in place.

Genus/species: *Reseda lutea, R. alba*

Common name: mignonette, white upright mignonette

Annual

Region: native to Africa; grown in temperate garden zones

Color: white, yellow, blue

Height: 10 to 24 inches (25 to 60 centimeters)

Arrangement: long, thin spikes add perspective to dense arrangements, also good in fan-shaped groups

The long stalks of tiny flowers become thin spikes densely packed with seeds. Air-dry these spikes by hanging while they are still green. Gardeners living in zones nine and ten should plant these in the fall; those in other zones should wait until the spring to plant for late summer blooming.

WILLIAM S. MOYE

ROMAN SZOLKOWSKI

Genus/species: *Rhamnus cathartica,* var.

Common name: common buckthorn

Shrub

Region: native to Europe and Asia; naturalized throughout eastern U.S.

Color: blue-black berries

Height: up to 18 feet (5.4 meters)

Arrangement: attractive alone or mixed with white flowers

Most varieties of this dramatic shrub can be used dried, but be aware that the berries are poisonous. Dry the branches by standing them in water, then spray with polyurethane to hold the berries and give them a shine.

ANITA MARCI

Genus/species: *Rhus typhina*
Common name: staghorn sumac
Perennial shrub
Region: native to all parts of the eastern U.S.
Color: deep red berries
Height: up to 30 feet (9 meters)
Arrangement: used for dramatic color in larger bouquets

Sumac is a handsome shrub that thrives in poor soil and on old farms. The red clusters of berries remain throughout the winter, but they are best picked shortly after the bright-colored leaves have dropped in the fall. Large clusters can be broken and wired for use in smaller bouquets as well as on herb wreaths.

Genus/species: *Robinia pseudocacia, R. hispida*
Common name: black locust, bristly locust
Tree
Region: native to the eastern U.S., Pennsylvania through Georgia, but grows elsewhere
Color: dark brown pods
Height: as tall as 80 feet (24 meters)
Arrangement: wired pods useful in modern arrangements as as an accent in traditional styles

The black locust and its close relative, the bristly locust, have a fairly narrow natural range. But their attractive blooms and neat shape have made them an ornamental favorite, so they are now naturalized in a scattered fashion throughout the eastern half of the U.S. Black locust pods are between two and four inches (five and ten centimeters) long and are dark brown on the outside and nearly white within. Bristly locust pods are covered with very short, dense bristles, which give them a soft, furry look. As they dry, they twist open, forming interesting shapes. They may be used singly or wired in clusters for larger arrangements and are also useful in cone wreaths.

WILLIAM S. MOYE

Genus/species: *Rosa rugosa, R. centifolia, R. multiflora,* var.
Common name: rose
Perennial shrub
Region: native to North America; grown in all temperate garden zones
Color: red, pink, yellow, and white
Height: varieties up to 15 feet (4.5 meters)
Arrangement: reds useful with ferns and rich green foliage; pinks attractive with delicate spring flowers

There are so many varieties of native and hybrid roses that entire books are written about them. For drying, it is best to gather the climbing or wild roses when they are in the bud stage or just barely open. They air-dry beautifully on screens and are perfect for nosegays and wreaths. They may be wired into clusters for bouquets. Some of these varieties, such as *R. eglanteria,* the sweet briar rose, may be dried face up in sand or silica gel. All hybrid varieties may be dried in dessicants, but only the pinks retain a good color. Yellows fade to an attractive ivory, and deep reds become almost black. Another notable product of the wild roses are the hips, red fruit of varying sizes that appears after the roses have faded. These may be air-dried by hanging or standing, and they are a nice addition to holiday and harvest arrangements.

MARY CLOSE

ANITA MARCI

Genus/species: *Rudbeckia hirta, R. fulgida, R. triloba*
Common name: brown-eyed Susan, black-eyed Susan
Perennial and biennial
Region: native to North America
Color: yellow and brown
Height: 1 to 3 feet (30 to 90 centimeters)
Arrangement: combines nicely with Queen Anne's lace (see page 73); useful as an accent

The cheery sight of these bright flowers is a sign of summer in most parts of the U.S., where they were originally natives of the prairie. Dry them in sand or silica gel, or hang them to dry and remove the petals, using the cone-shaped centers as accents in light-colored bouquets.

Genus/species: *Rumex acetosa,* var.
Common name: dock
Perennial
Region: grows wild throughout North America
Color: rose, green, tan, and rust
Height: 1 to 4 feet (30 to 120 centimeters)
Arrangement: spikes used for dramatic accent

Dock is so common, so easy to spot, and so attractive in bouquets, that it may indeed be the best-loved weed in America! Its seedheads can be picked at various times of the year for a whole range of colors from a pink-tinged tan through dark brown. In areas where snow makes wild gathering a strictly seasonal matter, the tall heads of dock are often visible above the snow. Since they are so sturdy, simply stand the green or pink spikes in a dry vase or hang them to dry. Or pick when already dry.

ANITA MARCI

Genus/species: *Ruscus aculeatus*
Common name: butcher's-broom
Evergreen shrub
Region: native to Europe; grown in U.S., south of garden zone 7
Color: green
Height: 18 to 48 inches (45 to 120 centimcters)
Arrangement: valuable as foliage and filler in any style of arrangement

Ruscus is such a beautiful, rich green, especially when glycerin-treated, that one wonders why florists are so fond of dyeing it bright red. It is a highly useful filler, usually available from florists.

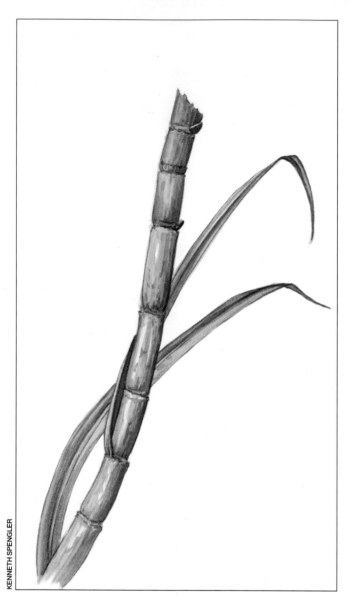

KENNETH SPENGLER

Genus/species: *Saccharum officinarum*
Common name: sugarcane
Perennial
Region: warm areas worldwide; grows throughout southern U.S.
Color: dries to buff
Height: 10 to 20 feet (3 to 6 meters)
Arrangement: good for large arrangements

The economic importance of sugarcane has led to its spread, and now these feathery, upright stems are grown in many parts of the world. The plumes contain hundreds of small spikes, so they are particularly good fillers. Air-dry sugarcane by standing it in a dry container.

Genus/species: *Salix discolor*
Common name: pussy willow
Perennial shrub
Region: native to eastern and
central U.S.
Color: silver, also available in pink
Height: up to 25 feet (7.6 meters)
Arrangement: perfect accent for
spring and woodland arrange-
ments, particularly with dried
narcissus (see page 131)

Catkins of pussy willow are among
the first treasures of spring and are
usually found at the edges of low,
moist areas and streams swollen from
the spring melt-off. Air-dry the
branches by standing them in a dry
vase. The stems of this willow are
soft and make good false stems for
flowers that have been dried in sand
with pins inserted in their bases.

KENNETH SPENGLER

KENNETH SPENGLER

Genus/species: *Salvia officinalis*
Common name: common sage,
garden sage
Perennial
Region: Mediterranean native;
grown in garden zones 3
through 10
Color: pale green, variegated with
yellow, white, and purple
Height: 1 to 3 feet (30 to 90
centimeters)
Arrangement: used in herb and
culinary wreaths

The long, oval pebbly surfaced
leaves of sage take on interesting
curls when dry. It is often combined
with artemisia (see page 32) as the
base for herb wreaths or with bay as
the base for kitchen wreaths. In either case it should be shaped while
fresh, since it tends to become brittle
when dry.

KENNETH SPENGLER

Genus/species: *Salvia splendens*
Common name: salvia, scarlet sage
Tender perennial and annual
Region: garden zones 3 through 10
Color: red
Height: 8 to 30 inches (20 to 75
centimeters)
Arrangement: used heavily in
Williamsburg-style arrangements

Although the intense red of the fresh flower darkens a little after drying in sand or silica gel, it still remains a fine flower for drying. It is grown as an annual only in garden zones three through eight. In American Colonial Williamsburg, scarlet sage was air-dried by hanging, and the resulting deep red was a dramatic mainstay of the fan-shaped and larger, showy arrangements.

Genus/species: *Sanguisorba minor*
Common name: salad burnet
Perennial
Region: garden zones 3 through 10 except Gulf Coast
Color: seedheads green to reddish purple
Height: 1 to 2 feet (30 to 60 centimeters)
Arrangement: leaves good in miniatures; seedheads useful anywhere

The delicate leaves of this salad herb grow in even pairs on fragile stems, and they are very attractive when pressed. The seedheads form from flowers that grow in early summer. Allow these to dry on the plant until bad weather threatens, then air-dry them on screens. The leaves are so hardy that they may be found bright and green under the first light snowfalls in the northern U.S.

WILLIAM S. MOYE

MARY CLOSE

Genus/species: *Scabiosa caucasica*
Common name: pincushion flower
Perennial
Region: native to Europe; grown in garden zones 3 through 10
Color: blue, mauve, pink, crimson, and white
Height: 2 feet (60 centimeters)
Arrangement: most appropriate for larger arrangements, but the flowers' centers may be used in smaller ones

The name of this plant comes from its shape, which features stamens standing out from the center of a cluster of petals. It is a favorite in English gardens, and can be dried in sand. When the petals wither, either in a fresh bouquet or on the plant, they may be removed to leave the oval, feathery center, which may be further dried by hanging. An annual variety of the same genus, *S. atropurpurea*, may be used in the same ways.

Genus/species: Scabiosa stellata
Common name: starflower, star
  everlasting
Annual
Region: grown in all temperate
  zones
Color: white and blue flowers turn
  pale green and bronze
Height: 18 to 24 inches (45 to 60
  centimeters)
Arrangement: blends well with any
  style, but is especially nice with
  feathery spikes such as astilbe or
  spiraea (see page 35)

After the petals fall from this
flower, a globe remains, made up of
numerous florets, each with a dark
star-shaped center. They dry on the
plant, with long, straight stems that
are sturdy and easy to work with in
arrangements.

KENNETH SPENGLER

KENNETH SPENGLER

Genus/species: *Schinus molle*
Common name: pepper tree,
pepperberries
Tree
Region: native to South America;
grows in California and the U.S.
South
Color: rose
Height: 15 to 25 feet (4.5 to 7.6
meters)
Arrangement: berries give a
refreshing variety to texture of
formal or Victorian massed
arrangements

Clusters of rose-colored berries are
the fruit of this weeping evergreen.
Cut the stems when the berries are at
their peak of color, remove the
leaves, and hang each stem to dry
separately. They can then be used in
large clumps or wired in small clusters along a stem to create drooping
racemes, which are very effective in
Victorian styles.

Genus/species: *Schinus
terebinthifolius*
Common name: wilelaiki,
Christmas-berry tree
Shrub and tree
Region: native to Brazil; also grows
in Hawaii
Color: white flowers; bright red
berries
Height: to 15 feet (4.5 meters)
Arrangement: useful in dramatic
arrangements for intense color;
also good with deep greens in
holiday settings

The flowers of Christmas-berry
trees develop into bright red fruit on
trees growing in dense thickets. Pick
the berries when they are fully colored, and hang them in separate clusters to dry. They last for years and
hold their color very well.

WILLIAM S. MOYE

Genus/species: *Sedum spectabile,*
   S. album
Common name: sedum
Perennial
Region: garden zones 3 through 10
Color: ivory, pink, and red
Height: up to 18 inches (45
   centimeters)
Arrangement: used as filler and for
   texture in backgrounds

Sedum does not look like a good
plant for drying, with its succulent-
appearing leaves, but the flowers actually dry quite well. Pick them at
the height of bloom and hang them to
dry. Seedheads of summer-blooming
varieties may be left on the plant to
dry.

ANITA MARCI

KENNETH SPENGLER

Genus/species: *Senecio cineraria*
Common name: dusty miller
Annual and perennial
Region: native to southern Europe;
  grown in garden zones 3
  through 10
Color: pale gray-green foliage
Height: 8 to 15 inches (20 to 38
  centimeters); as tall as 2.5 feet (76
  centimeters) in the U.S. South
Arrangement: combine with pale
  pink flowers and spikes of
  lavender for a misty, soft effect

Dusty miller grows as a perennial in
zones nine and ten. This plant's common name often causes confusion
with *Centaurea rutifolia* (see page
56), but both plants are used by arrangers in the same ways. They are
especially effective in gray and pink
Edwardian styles and in herbal
wreaths. Dry by pressing it lightly in
paper.

Genus/species: *Silene cucubalus*
Common name: bladder campion
Annual
Region: European native;
naturalized in U.S. from New
England to Kansas
Color: pale green and tan
Height: 12 to 18 inches (30 to 45
centimeters)
Arrangement: used as filler and
with whites

Too rangy a plant to be welcome in
the garden, campion is worth growing in a secluded corner for the in-
flated calyxes that are left when the
blossoms fall. These calyxes may be
picked early for a pale green color
that blends nicely with white and
pastel flowers in arrangements. Later
in the season it turns to a pale tan
that is useful in harvest bouquets.

ANITA MARCI

WILLIAM S. MOYE

Genus/species: *Smilacina
racemosa*
Common name: false Solomon's
seal
Perennial
Region: grows wild and is native to
most of North America
Color: white
Height: 1 to 3 feet (30 to 90
centimeters)
Arrangement: feathery plumes
make good fillers

A woodland plant, false Solomon's
seal has many small branches of tiny
white flowers that bloom in springtime. The feathery plumes may be
dried in sand and left on their zigzag
stem or cut short and wired to a plain
stem.

MARY CLOSE

Genus/species: *Solidago sempervirens, S. canadensis,* var.
Common name: goldenrod
Perennial
Region: native to North America; species grown in garden zones 3 through 10
Color: yellow
Height: 3 to 5 feet (90 to 150 centimeters)
Arrangement: used with grasses for wild arrangements or in herb wreaths; a good accent with darker flowers

The goldenrod is so common in nearly every part of North America that Americans are often surprised to see it in European seed catalogs. It has a bad name here quite unjustly, for it is usually blamed for the allergic reactions many people have to ragweed, which blooms at the same time and in most of the same places. Pick goldenrod when only about a third of the blossoms are open, and air-dry it by hanging. Pick it at different stages for other effects, but at this point the yellow flowers will remain much the same as when they were fresh. Tips of this combine well with grass heads and strawflowers on herb wreaths as well as in harvest bouquets.

Genus/species: *Sophora chrysophylla*
Common name: mamani, mamane
Shrub and tree
Region: native to China; found in Hawaii
Color: yellow flowers; brown pods
Height: to 40 feet (12 meters)
Arrangement: used singly or in clusters for a dramatic touch in modern arrangements

The bright yellow clusters of mamani flowers are shaped like the sweet pea, to which it is related. The flowers give way to winged seedpods up to six inches (fifteen centimeters) long, first green, then turning to brown. Pick them when they are brown, then wire them into upright clusters or use them singly.

WILLIAM S. MOYE

KENNETH SPENGLER

Genus/species: *Sorghum vulgare technicum*
Common name: broomcorn
Annual
Region: grown in temperate and subtropical garden zones
Color: tan and buff
Height: 4 to 6 feet (1.2 to 1.8 meters)
Arrangement: best in informal and wild bouquets

Stiff branches of these flower heads have been grown for centuries for use in broom making. They are attractive in harvest bouquets, and they provide long sweeping ends for swags, as well as sturdy backgrounds for fan-shaped arrangements. The Gurney Seed Company offers seeds for broomcorn, which could be difficult to obtain.

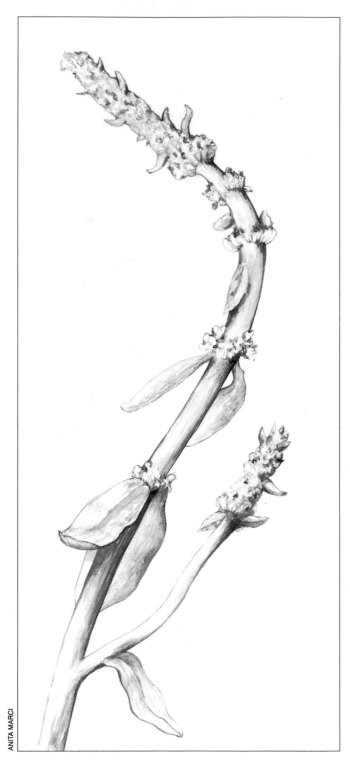

ANITA MARCI

Genus/species: *Stachys olympica;* syn. *S. lantana*

Common name: lamb's ears; wooly betony

Perennial

Region: grown in zones 3 through 10 except on Gulf Coast

Color: pink flowers; gray-green leaves

Height: 1 to 1.5 feet (30 to 45 centimeters)

Arrangement: used as accent in herb wreaths; combines attractively with hydrangea, lavender clusters, artemesia, and tiny blue larkspur

All parts of this plant are covered by a soft coating of tiny hairs, which give it a wooly appearance. Dry flower stalks just before they reach full bloom. Hang some to air-dry and lay others on a screen to preserve the interesting curves. Dry individual leaves on a screen for use in wreaths or for wiring in clumps for arrangements. The thick spikes are a good addition to a white and silver bouquet.

Genus/species: *Strelitzia reginae*
Common name: bird-of-paradise
Perennial
Region: native to South Africa;
 grows in California
Color: orange or yellow flowers;
 leaves dry to silver shade
Height: up to 18 feet (5.5 meters)
Arrangement: used as strong,
 exotic elements in contemporary
 designs

The dramatic blossoms of this plant do not dry well, but the leaves take on strange sculptural shapes when allowed to air-dry. Since they are quite heavy, they may require a month or more to fully dry. The shapes of the dried leaves can act as a framework around which to build a design.

WILLIAM S. MOYE

Genus/species: *Styphelia tameiameiae, S. douglasii*
Common name: pukiawe
Perennial shrub
Region: Hawaii
Color: white, pink, red, and maroon berries
Height: 1 to 3 feet (30 to 90 centimeters)
Arrangement: attractive wired in clusters for wreaths; useful in almost any style of arrangement because of its attractive texture and color

This branching shrub is found from as low as sea level to craters over 6000 feet (1800 meters) in altitude. Its small, leathery leaves have a whitish undersurface that dries to a dull gray-green, and they should be dried with the berries because they look nicer with the leaves. Pukiawe figures heavily in local folklore, and the berries are used in leis by the Hawaiians.

Genus/species: *Tagetes erecta, T.
   patula*
Common name: marigold
Annual
Region: grows in all zones
Color: orange; yellow
Height: 6 to 24 inches (15 to 60
   centimeters)
Arrangement: used for dramatic
   bursts of color, especially in
   autumn arrangements

Marigolds are the mainstay of the
annual border, where they may even
be planted from seed in moderate climates. In cooler zones, they should
be started indoors or purchased in
flats. They bloom profusely all summer if the blossoms are regularly
picked, so collecting them for drying
actually increases their beauty in the
garden. Insert a wire up through the
hollow stem into the flower head before hanging to dry. Smaller varieties
may be dried in silica gel or sand,
which prevents shrinking. These may
be mounted on artificial stems later if
about 1 inch (2.5 centimeters) of original stem is left attached. If the petals
seem loose in the calyx, dribble a little diluted glue into the base. To dry
in dessicant, place flower in with the
head facing up and let sand or silica
gel run in from the sides to fill in the
spaces.

MARY CLOSE

ANITA MARCI

Genus/species: *Tanacetum vulgare*
Common name: tansy
Perennial
Region: native to North America
and United Kingdom
Color: yellow
Height: 2 to 5 feet (60 to 150
centimeters)
Arrangement: used in nearly every
style of dried arrangement for its
strong color and compact shape

The deeply cut, fern-like leaves
and clusters of compact yellow buttons of the tansy are old garden favorites. The plants can still be found
growing around abandoned farm-
houses—it used to be planted close to
the kitchen door to keep out ants.
Cut when the buttons are just coming
into full bloom and hang in bunches
to dry. Heads of tansy are good
accents on herb wreaths, too.

Genus/species: *Thalictrum
polygamum; T. diocium,* var.
Common name: meadow rue
Perennial
Region: native to eastern North
America; grows in zones 5
through 10
Color: mauve, white, and yellow
Height: 2 to 8 feet (60 to 240
centimeters)
Arrangement: cloud-like clusters of
flowers used as filler

Although most of the wild varieties
of *Thalictri* are too tall for the garden, there are several cultivated varieties well worth growing. These
species of Asian origin include *T. spe-
ciosum* and *T. aquilegifolium.* Pick
just before the peak of bloom and air-
dry hanging. If the flowers are left to
ripen on the plant, they are followed
by interesting seed clusters, which
are also attractive to arrangers.

ANITA MARCI

Genus/species: *Thymus vulgaris*
Common name: common thyme
Perennial
Region: native to the
Mediterranean; grown in
temperate garden zones
Color: pink or white blossoms
Height: 1 foot (30 centimeters)
maximum
Arrangement: dense foliage sprays
make good filler; vine-like stems
can be wound onto wreath frames
for a beautiful, fragrant base

A low, shrubby perennial, thyme
has been a favorite in herb gardens
for over 2000 years. The leaves of its
variegated varieties have silver to
white edges, which are even more
striking when dried. Its tiny leaves
are only one-quarter to one-half an
inch (one-half to a bit over one centi-
meter) long, and are most fragrant
just before the plant blooms in early
summer. Hang the stems to air-dry
unless you wish to shape them for a
wreath base.

KENNETH SPENGLER

WILLIAM S. MOYE

Genus/species: *Tragopogon pratensis, T. dubius, T. porrifolius*
Common name: goatsbeard, meadow salsify, salsify
Perennial
Region: native to Eurasia; grown in the Rocky Montains
Color: white, yellow, and light purple
Height: 1 to 4 feet (30 to 120 centimeters)
Arrangement: large seedheads attractive in larger arrangements

These species of goatsbeard were brought from Europe for their edible roots. The plants forms two- to three-inch (five-to-eight-centimeter) seedheads, which resemble dandelions, but are not as fragile. They last well if partially dried on the plant, then cut and air-dried. Spraying them lightly with artist's fixative makes them even more durable.

Genus/species: *Trifolium arvense*
Common name: rabbit's foot clover
Annual
Region: native to North America
Color: gray tinged with pink
Height: 8 to 12 feet (20 to 30 centimeters)
Arrangement: excellent for small arrangements and wreaths

Although the fluffy heads of this clover tend to shatter if left too long before picking, it is a very sturdy dried material if picked at the right stage. Look for it in waste areas and along street and road margins. It is well suited to dry, sandy areas of subsoil. Hang in loose bunches to dry. Another clover, *T. agrarium,* the yellow hop clover, may be harvested after the blossoms have turned to a reddish brown.

ANITA MARCI

Genus/species: *Triticum vulgare*
Common name: wheat
Annual
Region: grown throughout the
    temperate regions of North
    America
Color: dries to beige
Height: 2 to 5 feet (60 to 150
    centimeters)
Arrangement: seed spikes equally
    at home in formal and wild
    arrangements

Developed from Eurasian ances-
tors, wheat now occupies one-fifth
of the cultivated land in the world. It
is therefore one of the easiest dried
materials to find. Its erect, short seed
spikes have separate, distinct seeds
which form a compact, neat group.
For a freestanding harvest accent,
gather a thick bundle of wheat stalks
together and tie them with raffia or a
neutral-colored ribbon. Cut the
stems off evenly to form a flat base
and stand the arrangement on the cut
end.

WILLIAM S. MOYE

ANITA MARCI

Genus/species: *Tulipa,* var.
Common name: tulip
Perennial
Region: garden zones 3 through 10
Color: nearly every color
Height: 9 to 30 inches (23 to 75 centimeters)
Arrangement: used in spring garden bouquets; attractive combined with stock (see page 124) or larkspur and delphinium (see pages 63 and 74)

Although tulips are not an easy flower to dry successfully, they are well worth the effort for their large, bright blooms. Pick them just as they are coming out of the bud stage, while the blossoms are still firm and barely open at the top. Cut each stem to one inch (two and one-half centimeters) and push it into silica gel to stand it up. Then carefully fill and surround flower, working in even layers so that the shape of the petals remains perfect. When dry, these are easily attached to surrogate stems. Tulips left on the plant turn to an interesting seedpod early in the summer.

Genus/species: *Typha latifolia, T. angustifolia*
Common name: cattail
Perennial
Region: common throughout North America
Color: brown
Height: 4 to 8 feet (1.2 to 2.4 meters)
Arrangement: used as an accent in all styles of arrangements

Understandably popular with flower arrangers, cattails are easy to dry if picked at the right stage. Try to gather them while the male flower—the golden tassel on the upper part of the stem—is still in flower, which is just after they have matured. Air-dry them standing. If they are picked too late, they will turn to a puffy mass of airborne seeds as they dry. The leaves may be pressed for use in tropical arrangements.

MARY CLOSE

WILLIAM S. MOYE

Genus/species: *Vaccinium reticulatum*
Common name: ohelo
Perennial shrub
Region: Hawaii
Color: red flowers; orange and yellow berries
Height: 2 feet (60 centimeters)
Arrangement: useful in small arrangements or on herb wreaths; the rich red and pale green blend well with herb foliage and soft muted colors

This Hawaiian relative of the blueberry and leatherleaf (see page 57) is common in the Kilauea crater and along roadsides, and is considered sacred to the Hawaiian god Pele. Its round, firm leaves are usually less than one inch (two centimeters) long and cluster close to the stems. Pick the flowers at their peak and air-dry them by hanging.

Genus/species: *Verbascum thapsus, V. blattaria, V. phoeniceum*
Common name: mullein
Biennial and perennial
Region: garden zones 4 through 10
Color: yellow flowers; pale green foliage
Height: 4 to 6 feet (1.2 to 1.8 meters)
Arrangement: leaf rosettes used in wreaths; flower stalks make dramatic accents in large arrangements

Usually considered a weed, mullein is a large plant common to waste areas. It is a perennial in garden zones six through nine, but it self-sows easily in northern zones, where it is a biennial. The rosettes of leaves may be air-dried the first year and the flower stalks the second. The long stalks used to be saturated in oil and carried as torches. It is often grown in herb gardens, where it earned a place as a dye and medicinal plant. Most people prefer to gather it in the wild since it is so large.

ANITA MARCI

Genus/species: *Veronica incana, V. spicata,* var.

Common name: veronica, speedwell

Perennial

Region: garden zones 3 through 9

Color: pink, blue, and white

Height: 1 to 2 feet (30 to 60 centimeters)

Arrangement: delicate spikes perfect in spring arrangements or mixed with pinks and rosebuds (see pages 75 and 151)

The spikes of blossoms on all these varieties remain in bloom over a long period. Let the spikes bloom about halfway up before picking them to dry. They may be air-dried by hanging or placed on their sides in sand or silica gel. Leave on some of the gray-green foliage as well.

ANITA MARCI

ROMAN SZOLKOWSKI

Genus/species: *Verticorida nitens*
Common name: verticordia
Perennial shrub
Region: native to southwest
  Australia
Color: pink, yellow, and red
Height: 3 to 6 feet (90 to 180
  centimeters)
Arrangement: tiny flowers used in
  miniature arrangements

The small, fuzzy puffs of the verticordia flower arrive in U.S. markets
already dried and ready to use. They
are surprisingly sturdy material for
all their fragile appearance, and they
make good filler for larger arrangements if several stems are wired together into a bunch.

Genus/species: *Viola odorata, V.*
  tricolor
Common name: sweet violet,
  Johnny-jump-up
Perennial and biennial
Region: *V. odorata,* garden zones 5
  through 10; *V. tricolor,* garden
  zones 3 through 8
Color: white to violet; purple to
  yellow
Height: 4 to 8 inches (10 to 20
  centimeters)
Arrangement: fragile blooms and
  heart-shaped leaves best in
  miniature arrangements and dried
  nosegays

Thought to have originated in the
Andes Mountains, these flowers soon
spread to Europe and North America.
Although they are fragile, they are
well worth the trouble of drying for
their almost transparent grace. Place
them horizontally, face upward in
sand for about two weeks. Be sure to
keep the long stem, even though it
may have to be reinforced with fine
wire. Press the leaves lightly or dry
them in sand with the stems at an angle so that they may be used to frame
blossoms in a nosegay.

WILLIAM S. MOYE

Genus/species: *Wisteria sinensis,*
  W. floribunda
Common name: Chinese wisteria,
  Japanese wisteria
Perennial vine
Region: native to Asia; grows wild
  in southern U.S.; cultivated in
  temperate garden zones
Color: purple
Height: climbs to any height with
  support
Arrangement: curled, bean-like
  pods effective as accents in all
  styles, especially modern ones

Wisteria is an attractive ornamental vine with cascading clusters of purple blossoms. Both its corkscrew tendrils and its interesting curled pods are easily air-dried for later wiring on stems. The varieties that grow wild in the U.S. South have smooth pods, while the Oriental ones have fat, oblong, fuzzy pods up to ten inches (twenty-five centimeters) long. These remain fuzzy when dried.

WILLIAM S. MOYE

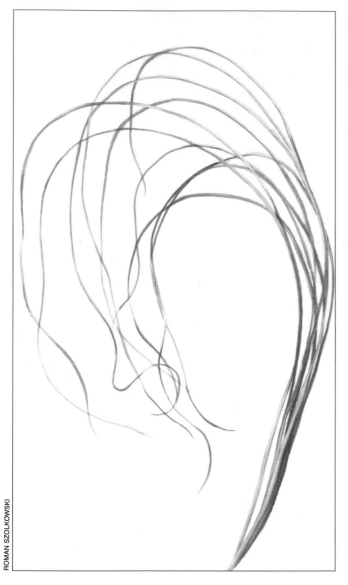

ROMAN SZOLKOWSKI

Genus/species: *Xerophyllum tenax*
Common name: bear grass, Indian
  basket grass
Perennial
Region: native to western U.S.,
  especially mountain regions
Color: white flowers
Height: 2 to 6 feet (60 to 180
  centimeters)
Arrangement: soft, willowy leaves
  make good background and filler

Native Americans used the strong
leaves of bear grass to make baskets
and other woven articles. The leaves
are dried for use in arrangements by
standing clumps in a vase with about
two inches (five centimeters) of water. Its long, flowing curves make it
best for larger pieces, especially modern ones where unusual shapes are
desired.

Genus/species: *Yucca filamentosa,*
   Y. whipplei, var.
Common name: yucca, Adam's
   needle, Spanish bayonet,
   Our-Lord's-candle
Perennial
Region: native to the American
   Southwest; grown in garden zones
   6 through 10
Color: white
Height: 3 to 6 feet (90 to 180
   centimeters)
Arrangement: entire spikes of
   seedpods, or individual dried
   blossoms, useful in nearly any
   style of arrangement

While it is usually not considered hardy north of garden zone six, there are some lovely specimens of yucca growing in zone five gardens, so northern gardeners should not be afraid to try their luck with this versatile plant. Pick individual blossoms close to the central stem and dry them face up in sand or silica gel. They will become almost transparent and should be sprayed lightly with floral fixative to protect them from moisture. Wire them to stems singly or in clusters. The yucca's dried seedpods may also be wired in clusters or individually, but they are most dramatic when left on their stems and used in large, modern arrangements. The leaves are tough and have an abundance of curled white fibers growing out of the edges. They airdry easily and are also very attractive in arrangements.

WILLIAM S. MOYE

Genus/species: *Zantedeschia aethiopica*
Common name: calla lily
Perennial
Region: native to tropical Africa; cultivated in tropical gardens elsewhere
Color: white
Height: up to 30 inches (75 centimeters)
Arrangement: perfect as the focal point in modern or large arrangements

A beautiful white spathe up to ten inches (twenty-five centimeters) long enfolds the base of a striking spadix. These flowers dry beautifully if placed face up in a deep container of sand. Dry the arrowhead-shaped leaves too, by pressing, hanging, or watering. Florists frequently offer the blooms as cut flowers.

Genus/species: *Zea mays*
Common name: corn
Annual
Region: garden zones 4 through 10
Color: yellow, red, and blue ears
Height: up to 15 feet (4.5 meters)
Arrangement: braid husks for door decorations; small ears combine well with grasses for harvest arrangements

There are many varieties of ornamental corn, including Indian, blue and strawberry. In some cases, the husks are colored as well. Although sweet corn may be grown in northern zones, the drying varieties need a longer season in order to dry on the stalk; many require one hundred days of a frost-free growing season. Larger ears may be used in braids, while the small ears are wired to stems for use in arrangements. Peel back the husks to dry them in a radiating position like flower petals. Corn tassels are popular in Williamsburg-style arrangements, and the leaves may also be dried for foliage in large-scale arrangements.

ROMAN SZOLKOWSKI

Genus/species: *Zinnia elegans*
Common name: zinnia
Annual
Region: native to Mexico; garden
zones 3 through 10
Color: red, pink, yellow, orange,
and white
Height: 1 to 3 feet (30 to 90
centimeters)
Arrangement: used for vibrant
splashes of color in summer
bouquets

Zinnias are among the most popular garden flowers, and the same qualities make them popular with arrangers. They are long-lasting, brightly colored, and nicely shaped both in gardens and in bouquets. They are easily dried in silica gel or sand, and the slightly hollow stems can be cut short and placed on any stiff straw or stem after drying. Zinnias may be air-dried by suspending them on a wire mesh with the stems hanging downward. The shape of the flower will change in this process, but the vibrant colors will remain.

MARY CLOSE

SOURCES FOR COMMON PLANTS AND SEEDS

ADAMS NURSERY
Box 606, Route 20
Westfield, MA 01086
(413) 736-0443

APPLEWOOD SEED CO.
5380 Vivian Street
Arvada, CO 80002
(303) 431-6283

ARROWHEAD GARDENS
115 Boston Post Road
Wayland, MA 01778
(617) 358-7333

BACHMAN'S INC.
6010 Lyndale Avenue South
Minneapolis, MN 55419
(612) 861-7600

W. ATLEE BURPEE CO.
300 Park Avenue
Warminster, PA 18974
(215) 674-4900

BUSSE GARDENS
Route 2, Box 238
Cokato, MN 55321
(612) 286-2654

CARROLL GARDENS
Box 310
Westminster, MD 21157
(301) 848-5422

THE CUMMINS GARDEN
22 Robertsville Road
Marlboro, NJ 07746
(201) 536-2591

EMLONG NURSERIES
2671 West Marquette Woods Rd.
Stevensville, MI 49127
(616) 429-3431

FARMER SEED AND NURSERY
818 Northwest 4th Street
Faribault, MN 55021
(507) 334-6421

EARL FERRIS NURSERY
811 4th Street, NE
Hampton, IA 50441
(515) 456-2563

HENRY FIELD SEED AND
NURSERY CO.
407 Sycamore Street
Shenandoah, IA 51602
(605) 665-9391

GARDENS OF THE BLUE
RIDGE
Box 10
Pineola, NC 28662
(704) 733-2417

C.M. HOBBS & SONS
9300 West Washington Street
Box 31227
Indianapolis, IN 46231
(317) 241-9253

INTER-STATE NURSERIES
Box 135
Hamburg, IA 51644
(712) 382-2411

JUNG SEED CO.
335 South High Street
Randolph, WI 53957
(414) 326-3121

KEIL BROTHERS
220-15 Horace Harding Blvd.
Bayside, NY 11364
(718) 224-2020

KELLY BROTHERS NURSERIES
Dansville, NY 14437
(716) 335-2211

KIMBERLY BARN FLORAL
AND GARDEN CENTER
1221 East Kimberly Road
Davenport, IA 52807
(319) 386-1300

LITTLEFIELD-WYMAN
NURSERIES
227 Centre Avenue
Abington, MA 02351
(617) 878-1800

LOUISIANA NURSERY
Route 7, Box 43
Opelousas, LA 70570
(318) 948-3696

LAMB NURSERIES
East 101 Sharp Avenue
Spokane, WA 99202
(509) 328-7956

McCLURE & ZIMMERAN
1422 West Thorndale
Chicago, IL 60660
(312) 989-0557

EARL MAY SEED AND
NURSERY CO.
Shenandoah, IA 51603
(712) 246-1020

MELLINGER'S
2310 West South Range Road
North Lima, OH 44452
(216) 549-9861

MOON MOUNTAIN
WILDFLOWERS
P.O. Box 34
Morro Bay, CA 93442
(805) 772-2473

NEOSHO NURSERIES
1020 North College
Neosho, MO 64850
(417) 451-1212

NUCCIO'S NURSERIES
3555 Chaney Trail
Altadena, CA 91001
(213) 259-5609

L.L. OLDS SEEDS CO.
2901 Packers Avenue
Madison, WI 53704
(608) 249-9291

ORLANDO'S PRIDE
NURSERIES
145 Weckerly Road
Butler, PA 16001
(412) 283-0962

GEORGE W. PARK SEED CO.
Greenwood, SC 29647
(803) 374-3341

POWELL'S GARDENS
Route 3, Box 21
Princeton, NC 27569
(919) 936-4421

PUTNEY NURSERY
Box 265
Putney, VT 05346
(802) 387-5577

ROSEDALE NURSERIES
Saw Mill River Parkway
Hawthorne, NY 10532
(914) 769-1300

ROSES OF YESTERDAY AND
TODAY
802 Brown's Valley Road
Watsonville, CA 95076
(408) 724-3537

SCARFF'S NURSERY
Route 1
Carlisle, OH 45344
(513) 845-3130

SEVEN DEES NURSERY
16519 Southeast Stark
Portland, OR 97233
(503) 255 9225

SHEPHERD'S GARDEN SEEDS
7389 West Zayante Road
Felton, CA 95018
(408) 335-5400

SILVER FALLS NURSERY AND
CHRISTMAS TREE FARM
Silver Falls Highway
Star Route, Box 84
Silverton, OR 97381
(503) 873-4945

THOMPSON & MORGAN
P.O. Box 1308
Jackson, NJ 08527
(201) 363-2225

SOURCES FOR
EQUIPMENT AND
SUPPLIES

GALERIE FELIX FLOWER
968 Lexington Avenue
New York, NY 10021
(212) 772-7701

GARDENER'S EDEN
Williams-Sonoma
P.O. Box 7307
San Francisico, CA 94120
(415) 421-4242

BEATRICE MANN FLORIST
150 Central Park South
New York, NY 10019
(212) 757-1790

PEOPLE'S FLOWER
CORPORATION
786 6th Avenue
New York, NY 10001
(212) 686-6291

PLANTABBS CORPORATION
P.O. Box 397
Timonium, MD 21093
(301) 252-4620

RIALTO FLORIST INC.
707 Lexington Avenue
New York, NY 10022
(212) 688-3234

RICHARD SALOME FLOWERS
152 East 79th Street
New York, NY 10021
(212) 988-2933

SMITH & HAWKEN
25 Corte Madera
Mill Valley, CA 94941
(415) 383-4050

SOURCES FOR UNUSUAL
PLANTS AND SEEDS

THE BANANA TREE
715 Northhampton Street
Easton, PA 18042
(215) 253-9589

THE BOVEES NURSERY
1737 Southwest Coronado
Portland, OR 97219
(503) 244-9341

EXOTICA SEEDS
2508-B East Vista Way
P.O. Box 160
Vista, CA 92083
(619) 724-9093

GURNEY SEED AND NURSERY
CO.
Yankton, SD 57079
(605) 665-4451

JOSEPH J. KERN ROSE
NURSERY
Box 33
Jackson Street and Heisley
Road
Mentor, OH 44060
(216) 255-8627

PLANTS OF THE SOUTHWEST
1812 Second Street
Sante Fe, NM 87501
(505) 983-1548

CLYDE ROBIN
Box 2366
Castro Valley, CA 94546
(415) 581-3468

SALTER TREE FARM
Route 2, Box 1332
Madison, FL 32340
(904) 973-6312

ANTHONY J. SKITTONE
1415 Eucalyptus
San Francisco, CA 94132
(415) 753-3332

THOMPSON & MORGAN
P.O. Box 1308
Jackson, NJ 08527
(201) 363-2225

RECOMMENDED
FIELD GUIDES

Peterson, Roger Tory, and
  Margaret McKenney. *A Field
  Guide to Wildflowers.*
  Boston: Houghton-Mifflin
  Co., 1986.

Stokes, Donald. *A Guide to
  Nature in Winter.* Boston:
  Little, Brown and Co., 1976.

CROSS-REFERENCE OF BOTANICAL AND COMMON PLANT NAMES